Virtuous Woman Take Your Place In Destiny

LUCY S. PARRY

Most Bible passages used in this book are from "The Message" version - therefore referring to other versions of the Bible is recommended.

Order this book online at www.trafford.com/04-0460
or email orders@trafford.com

Most Trafford titles are also available at major online book retailers.

Note for Librarians: A cataloguing record for this book is available from Library and Archives Canada at www.collectionscanada.ca/amicus/index-e.html

ISBN: 978-1-4120-2632-1

We at Trafford believe that it is the responsibility of us all, as both individuals and corporations, to make choices that are environmentally and socially sound. You, in turn, are supporting this responsible conduct each time you purchase a Trafford book, or make use of our publishing services. To find out how you are helping, please visit www.trafford.com/responsiblepublishing.html

Our mission is to efficiently provide the world's finest, most comprehensive book publishing service, enabling every author to experience success. To find out how to publish your book, your way, and have it available worldwide, visit us online at www.trafford.com/10510

www.trafford.com

North America & international
toll-free: 1 888 232 4444 (USA & Canada)
phone: 250 383 6864 • fax: 250 383 6804
email: info@trafford.com

The United Kingdom & Europe
phone: +44 (0)1865 722 113 • local rate: 0845 230 9601
facsimile: +44 (0)1865 722 868 • email: info.uk@trafford.com

10 9 8 7 6 5 4

Dedicated to

My Prayer Partners
May God by His infinite Wisdom lead you all step by step
till you discover your purposes in life

Contents

Acknowledgements

With special thanks

- To my husband - George; for making it possible for me to write this book. It has been eighteen years full of challenges but I thank God for the heart He gave you for our family. Thank you very much for your love and support.

- My special thanks also goes to all the Pastors, Leaders and the whole congregation of The Redeem Christian Church of God – House of Praise, London network for your love.

- To my mentor - Deaconess Jessie Sampar; for your words of encouragement and prayers. Thank you very much for your enthusiasm about this book and your consistently positive input. May God richly bless you!

- To my prayer partners - for all your love and encouragements. Thank you for sharing your lives experiences with me; may God, who has started this good work in you, provide for you and bring you to a perfect ending.

Foreword

Virtuous Woman is a revelation, received in prayer and by reading the Bible to encourage different types of women in our society and in this world. The present age is full of evil; Satan and his agents are doing everything possible to discourage the virtuous woman from achieving her God-given goals and fulfilling her destiny.

First and foremost, this book is a source of encouragement for the woman who has not fully understood the plan and purposes for her life. To this woman God is saying; "Before you were even formed in your mother's womb, I knew you!" *"Never will I leave you; never will I forsake you" [Hebrews 13:5]. NIV*

Secondly, it is a source of encouragement for the woman who, due to circumstances beyond her control, has separated from the man to whom she was once married. To this woman God is saying; " Get to know me, read my word and encourage yourself, all is not lost and it is not yet over! *"All things work together for good,* [fitted into a plan] *for those who love God and are called according to His design and purpose." [Romans 8:28]. NIV*

Finally, it is also a source of encouragement for women who are being persecuted because of their faith. To these women God is saying; "Don't faint, be courageous. Run the race and win by holding on to my promises and taking members of your household with you". *"For those who trust in the Lord for help, will find their strength renewed. They will rise on wings like eagles; they will run and not get weary; they will walk and not grow weak" [Isaiah 40:31].*

Women from all walks of life, whether married or single, should be made aware of the extent of God's love for mankind. The book of John states; " *God loved the world so much that He gave his only Son to die on the Cross, so that anyone who believes in him may not die but have eternal life" [John 3:16].* Believe it or not, The Creator had you in mind when He created this world.

This very moment, you may be living with rejection, frustration and pain, which you feel you can't share with anyone else. But don't be discouraged. God is saying; "*My power is made perfect in your weakness.*" [2 Corinthians 12:9], which means, once you have realised your human limitations, you may feel inadequate to carry on with life – but don't give up hope because that is when God releases more of His power, to sustain you.

Remember, anyone the world looks down on, considers weak, and despises; she is the exact person The Creator chooses to confound the wise and powerful [1 Corinthians 1:27]. NIV

To attain your God-given potentials

Choose to be different if it will help you to achieve your goals.
Choose to associate with people who believe in your dreams.
Chose to go where you are celebrated instead of abused.
Choose to be at peace with anyone who comes your way.

Choose to be the best in your own field.
Choose to love people unconditionally.
Choose to be happy because you only ever live once.
Choose to believe that all things are possible to those who have faith in God.

The conception and birth of our Lord Jesus gives an inclination of the "power" endowed to women. Just as Mary, [mother of Jesus] conceived through the power of the Holy Spirit, women are also receptive to vital revelations from the Holy Spirit.

The birth of Jesus

"Now the birth of Jesus Christ took place under these circumstances: When His mother Mary had been promised in marriage to Joseph, before they came together, she was found to be pregnant [through the power] of the Holy Spirit."[Matthew 1:18]

An *Angel appeared to Joseph in a dream and said, "she will bear a Son, and you shall call His name* Jesus [the Greek form of the Hebrew Joshua, which means Saviour], *for He will save His people from their sins* [that is, prevent them from failing and missing the true end and scope of life, which is God]. *[Matthew 1: 21]*

Jesus, conceived through the power of the Holy Spirit, a symbol of hope for the world, was born to be a solution to a problem. This means for women to deliver solutions to problems, just like Mary, The Holy Spirit will have to be actively involved in their decision making [not their husbands alone].

Women have been created to possess the following powers:

- Power to conceive positive ideas in the spiritual realm.
- Power to nurture this new hope until delivery.
- Power to go through physical, biological and spiritual transformations.
- Power to travail.
- Power to be influential.
- Power to cater for needs.

Women who do not channel their creative powers wisely initiate most problems in this world. Embedded deep within each woman are vital ideas to solve most domestic issues of life. There is a saying, "A *woman is the worst enemy of another woman*". This is not just a myth because women by nature possess special powers to either build or destroy.

Power of a woman [which needs to be utilised positively]

- It is only a woman who can tell the actual time and day her baby was conceived.
- The initial decision to carry pregnancy through comes from a woman.
- It is only a woman who can identify the true father of her child.
- Women can tolerate and endure unpleasant experiences in marriage to prevent separation or divorce.
- Decisions to prevent extra-marital affairs lies with another woman.

- Women, in most cases, determine the menu for the family.
- Most women are multi-tasked when it comes to responsibilities.
- Women usually care for their children and spouses.

To activate her creative powers positively, the woman needs to do one thing, and that is to acknowledge God and accept His love. It is only through the power of the Holy Spirit that the woman can 'conceive' ideas, which could bring solutions to problems she encounters at home, in her community, in church, and perhaps even on a larger scale.

Women should understand that fullness of joy is only found in Him [God]. His Word declares; "*The thief,* [the devil] *comes only in order to steal, kill and destroy. But Jesus came that we may have and enjoy life, and have it in abundance*". *[John 10:10]*

Jesus is also known as the Word of God [or the Bible], so for the woman to possess her God-given powers she has to make the Bible her friend.

It does not matter what circumstances you might find yourself in, nor does it matter whether you are about to check-out from this experience known as "life on earth", into life eternal [the unknown]; for the assurance He [Jesus] is offering is not for this life alone, it is for life everlasting.

Virtuous woman, wherever you go and whatever you do, The Creator wants you to acknowledge Him and to have daily fellowship with Him. One thing you have to bear in mind—you have embarked on a journey to a certain destination. The ball is in your court and the choice is entirely yours; whether you want to make the journey of life alone, or with a friend who can assist by giving you strength to overcome challenges and obstacles life might throw your way.

This passage, from the Song of Songs, is a meditation for the virtuous woman who wants to win her home for the Lord Jesus Christ. It is also a source of encouragement, for the single woman to look up to Jesus in times of loneliness and doubt. For God has not given us a fearful spirit, rather He gave us the gifts of love, strength and free will to choose.

"I hear my lover's voice.
He comes running over the mountains,
racing across the hills to me.
My lover is like a gazelle, like a young stag.
There he stands beside the wall.
He looks in through the window
and glances through the lattice.
My lover speaks to me.
Come then my love; my darling, come with me.
The winter is over the rains have stopped.
In the countryside the flowers are in bloom.
This is the time for singing;
the song of doves is heard in the fields.
My lover is mine, and I am his.
He feeds his flock among the lilies
until the morning breezes blow
and the darkness disappears.
Return my darling, like a gazelle,

Like a stag on the mountains of Bether.
Asleep on my bed, night after night
I dreamt of the one I love;
I was looking for him but couldn't find him.
I went wandering through the city,
through its streets and alleys.
I looked for the one I love.
I looked, but couldn't find him.
The watchmen patrolling the city saw me.
I asked them, "Have you found my lover?"
As soon as I left them, I found him.
I held him and wouldn't let him go
until I took him to my mother's house,
to the room where I was born" .
{Song of Songs 2:8-12, 3:1-4}

Chapter One

THE TWO FOUNDATIONS OF LIFE
IGNORANCE
LAZINESS
CARELESSNESS

Women in today's Society are faced with countless challenges and pressures of life. Pressure from home, work or the community can mount up so high, to a point where it is difficult to know where to turn. The good news I have for such a woman is that you don't have to suffer in silence any longer. You can have a friend who will see you through this state of hopelessness.

With The Lord on your side, you are guaranteed a friend who is always there, to hold your hand through thick and thin. The word of God tells us; "*Be strong and courageous. Do not be afraid or terrified, for the LORD your God, who is All Mighty, All Powerful and Everlasting, goes with you*".

The Creator is also saying; "*Can a mother forget the baby at her breast and have no compassion on the child she has born? Though she may forget, I will not forget you! See, I have engraved you on the palms of my hands; your walls are ever before me.*" *[Isaiah 49:15-16].*

TIPS

1. Acknowledging you are not a result of an accident: but rather you are "fearfully and wonderfully" made will give you hope to carry on with life if you are over-burdened.
2. Accepting that the one who created you is head over heels in love with you will give you focus.
3. A simple act such as changing methods or ways of dealing with issues can make great impact and bring positive results if you desire a change.
4. Making a quality decision, of effectively handling certain issues of life before the issue in question ever present itself, will provide you with a better option and a good judgement.
5. If you do not believe in a Supreme Being, or a Higher Being, the fear of the unknown might prevent you from doing something tangible with your life.
6. Life is full of challenges but staying positive and having confidence in the good you believe in will definitely yield good results.

The word of God describes two types of women in this world: -

A "wise" woman and the "foolish". Typical examples are depicted in the following two parables:

THE TWO FOUNDATIONS OF LIFE

Parable 1

Jesus said, "Therefore everyone who hears these words of Mine and acts on them, may be compared to a wise [woman or man] who built [her] house on the rock. The rain fell, and the floods came, and the winds blew and slammed against that house; and yet it did not fall, for it had been founded on the rock". [Matthew 7:24-25]

Parable 2

"Everyone who hears these words of Mine and does not act on them will be like a foolish [woman or man] who built [her] house on the sand. "The rain fell, and the floods came, and the winds blew and slammed against that house; and it fell—and great was its fall." [Matthew 7: 26-27] .

Jesus told this parable, to lay emphasis on the importance of using the principles of his teachings, as guide-lines for our choices in life.

The difference between the two women mentioned is mainly their choices when faced with a challenge: which on this occasion was building a house. They both had the ability to seek guidance from the teachings in the Bible of how a good house should be built. Both were also given "raw materials" necessary to achieve good results; but unlike the woman in our first parable, the second woman, of her own free will, decided not to follow the established principles to have the job done properly.

The factors that contributed to the fall of her "house" can be listed as follows:

- **Ignorance**
- **Laziness**
- **Carelessness**

IGNORANCE

(People perish for lack of knowledge)

Knowledge, as some people say, is power. Ecclesiastes in the Bible helps us to understand that there is nothing new under the sun and that ignorance is a device to keep people in bondage.

"What has been will be again, what has been done will be done again; there is nothing new under the sun. Is there anything of which one can say, "Look! This is something new"? It was here already, long ago; it was here before our time. There is no remembrance of men of old, and even those who are yet to come, will not be remembered by those who follow". [Ecclesiastes 1: 9-11]

Most solutions to problems pertaining to living a successful life have been discovered long before this generation came into existence, but human beings by nature prefer to learn from their own mistakes. Secondly, there are not enough trustworthy mentors in this day and age from which to learn. Prominent people in authority have received a new revelation which says, "Do as I tell you but don't look at my lifestyle." The Bible explain this issue as follows:

"You stumble day and night, and the prophets stumble with you. So I will destroy your mother. My people are destroyed from lack of knowledge. "Because you have rejected knowledge, I also reject you as my priests; because you have ignored the law of your God,

I also will ignore your children. The more the priests increased, the more they sinned against me; they exchanged their Glory for something disgraceful".[Hosea 4:5-7]NIV

TIPS

1. Listen to the advice of the elderly but never settle for their lifestyle.
2. Your breakthrough in life is determined by what you are prepared to learn.
3. Individual circumstances in life are not the same and as such knowledge needs to be applied with wisdom in any given situation.
4. Knowledge applied wisely brings solutions, so get understanding in whatever you are doing in life.
5. Never wait for the approval of anyone. Seek proper counselling and help if you need it.
6. Have a mentor or someone you can confide in because life can be very lonely at times.

LAZINESS

(Laziness can ruin your life, as you will not achieve your goals)

A lazy person always finds an excuse for why something cannot be done. There is a saying, "Where there is a will there is a way".

When it comes to "will power", time and finances to get certain things done do not come into the equation. Laziness in most cases is lack of direction, interest and motivation, but in life and destiny, if one is seeking for success, one cannot afford to overlook certain important issues. The Bible describe this as follows:

"How long will you lie there, you sluggard? When will you get up from your sleep? A little sleep, a little slumber, a little folding of the hands to rest and poverty will come on you like a bandit, and scarcity like an armed man". [Proverbs 6:9-11] NIV

TIPS

1. Most targets in life and destiny are achievable if one is willing to pay the price.
2. The cure for laziness is discovering your purpose in life.
3. Your assignment is determined by your passion, so if there is no one to encourage you, stay motivated and reach out for your dreams.
4. Blaming others for their inadequacies will not solve any problem but taking ownership of your life, will give you clear direction.
5. "Life" is what you make of it because it is directed and lived once by you.
6. Life on earth is temporal so you might as well make good use of it whilst it lasts.

CARELESSNESS

(Not paying attention to instructions from the Word of God)

Knowledge without its right application to a problem is useless.

Wisdom as somebody described it is, "right application of knowledge". What use is knowledge if its not applied wisely to bring a solution? People who are careless have an idea of how things should be done but are simply not prepared to pay the price to follow detailed instructions to accomplish that task. The Bible explain this as follows:

"For the Lord gives wisdom, and from his mouth come knowledge and understanding. He holds victory in store for the upright. He is a shield to those whose walk is blameless, for he guards the course of the just and protects the way of his

faithful ones. Then you will understand what is right and just and fair in every good path. For wisdom will enter your heart, and knowledge will be pleasant to your soul. Discretion will protect you, and understanding will guard you.

Wisdom will save you from the ways of wicked men, from men whose words are perverse, who leave the straight paths to walk in dark ways, who delight in doing wrong and rejoice in the perverseness of evil, whose paths are crooked and who are devious in their ways.

[Proverbs 2:6-15] NIV

TIPS

1. Success in what ever you do requires effort and determination.
2. Successful achievement comes in stages and you must be prepared to work towards it.
3. Failure is not denial. It simply means more effort needs to be applied.
4. Every situation in life is subject to change so never make a permanent decision based on temporal difficulties.
5. Trials and temptations, if endured to the end, bring maturity.
6. Take time and perform every duty with perfection. If not, it could cost you twice the expense and time to complete it.

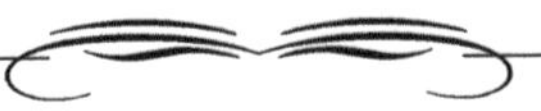

Chapter Two

SEASONS OF LIFE
UNDERSTANDING YOUR UNIQUENESS
TEAMWORK
PRIORITISING YOUR TIME

Through this journey of life on which you have embarked, you will be faced with many challenges, such as acquiring enough knowledge to stand on your feet as an individual person in society; choosing a career; getting married; raising children of your own; growing old; and finally, death. Each stage comes with its own challenges. Understanding the changing seasons of life and getting prepared in advance is of vital importance. The question is "How prepared are you for the next season in your life?"

Surely, if you are going to sit for an examination on any given subject, the day and time will come when you need to mention the source document from which you have acquired your knowledge. If your research is not based upon reading recognised textbooks, chosen by the examination board for the subject in question, unfortunately all your efforts and labour could be in vain.

On this journey there are so many different ways to equip yourself to face your next challenge. The only disadvantage is not equipping yourself with the necessary information and instructions in order to have the job done properly. Life is like a journey and because you are not stationed in one place, you might not always get the opportunity, or the time, to correct your mistakes. This is why the urgency to get the foundations right, at the beginning, should be your number one priority.

SEASONS OF LIFE

Life goes through many seasons. Getting yourself prepared at each stage is equally important. Using the word of God as your daily manual will instruct you and direct you clearly. Reading the word of God will not only instruct you, but also warn you against the danger of running ahead of time and not allowing each season to take its natural course.

The book of Genesis, for example, clearly defines the meaning of sex as a sacred intimacy between a married man and his wife. The Bible says; "*Therefore shall a man leave his father and mother and shall cleave unto his wife*: *and they shall be one flesh*" [Genesis 2:24].

A teenage girl, about to choose a career, if wise, will not waste the opportunities available to her by being promiscuous. Instead she will wait, reserving that sacred intimacy for her future husband, choosing rather to establish herself in the workplace first. The reason being, she understands the timing and she is also aware of the damage that such a careless attitude can cause – e.g. unwanted pregnancy, disease or even rushing into marriage with the wrong motive or with a man who could continuously cause her heartache for the rest of her life. The Book of Psalms explain the above as follows:

"I gain understanding from your precepts; therefore I hate every wrong path. Your word is a lamp to my feet and a light for my path. I have taken an oath and confirmed it, that I will follow your righteous laws. I have suffered much; preserve my life, O Lord, according to your word".[Psalm 119:104-107]NIV

In life, there are so many possible solutions to a problem but there might be only one, which is applicable to your needs. Acquiring knowledge is useful but right application of that concept to individual needs is essential.

TIPS

1. Make decisions, not based on people's opinion but on what is applicable to your specific needs.
2. Observe how a young lad treats elderly women [if respectfully] before accepting to go on a date with him.
3. Anyone who is not prepared to invest in a relationship does not deserve to have you as a companion.
4. The fact that something is working for others does not necessary mean it will work for you.
5. Power to succeed in whichever field you are in is determined by your own dreams. Others are simply there because they share a common dream as you.
6. You have been endowed with power to change circumstances that are not favourable, except in your commitments to God, so never be in haste

to take a partner to the altar: in doing that you are making a vow before God.

UNDERSTANDING YOUR UNIQUENESS

Understanding the word of God will help you, as an individual, to understand that you are unique in the world. Human comprehension cannot fully grasp how uniquely God, in His infinite wisdom, has created each individual. Each person has been created to perform a certain function. If you were to fail in the task given to you, whatever it may be, finding your replacement may not be possible. You are uniquely made! You are not replaceable; neither in your home, church, community nor in this world.

The Creator had our uniqueness in mind when He created human beings. He illustrated this by using the human body. The human body is extremely complex. If one limb or organ does not function correctly, the whole body is affected. This smaller picture can be translated into a bigger picture as God sees us. Each individual has been given an assignment, which can only be achieved by walking in love and unity with others.

For example, to create good music there has to be a composer, a lyricist, a good singer, guitarist, pianist, the drummer and many others. It is the responsibility of each individual who is part of that team to focus on what they have in common, not their differences. They must strive to work in unity, because they share a common purpose, which is to create a beautiful sound.

To work effectively in unity, team members have to magnify the strengths [good things] in people and not their weaknesses [bad things]. Everybody has their strengths and their weaknesses in life, and human beings, by nature, are drawn closer to people who accept and love them unconditionally.

The understanding and application of the simple rule described above would make great impact and achieve great results in our homes, communities, churches and throughout the world if everybody were to adopt it as a maxim for life.

TIPS

1. A productive team member is honest about her abilities and shortcomings.
2. She never turns everything to her own advantage but seek for the well being of other members in her team.
3. She is always eager to assist others and share vital information.
4. She is very secure in her abilities but does not give the impression that the team will not succeed without her input.
5. She is always kind and considerate when it comes to selecting who should stay behind to accomplish a task.
6. She is proactive and assertive to invest in new ideas to strengthen the team.

TEAMWORK

"The body is a unit, though it is made up of many parts; and though all its parts are many, they form one body. So it is with Christ. For we were all baptised by one Spirit into one body—whether Jews or Greeks, slave or free and we were all given the same Spirit to drink.

Now the body is not made up of one part but of many. If the foot should say, "Because I am not a hand, I do not belong to the body," it would not for that reason cease to be part of the body. And if the ear should say, "Because I am not an eye, I do not belong to the body," it would not for that reason cease to be part of the body. If the whole body were an eye, where would the sense of hearing be? If the whole body were an ear, where would the sense of smell be? But in fact God has arranged the parts in the body, every one of them, just as he wanted them to be. If they were all one part, where would the body be? As it is, there are many parts, but one body.

The eye cannot say to the hand, "I don't need you!" And the head cannot say to the feet, "I don't need you!" On the contrary, those parts of the body that seem to be weaker are indispensable, and the parts that we think are less honourable we treat with special honour. And the parts that are un-presentable are treated with special modesty, while our presentable parts need no special treatment. But God has combined the members of the body and has given greater honour to the parts that lacked it, so that there should be no division in the body, but that its parts should have equal concern for each other. If one part suffers, every part suffers with it; if one part is honoured, every part rejoices with it. [1 Corinthians 12:12-26]

Understanding your uniqueness will assist you to find your place as a valuable team member. It will also help you to understand that your "seasons of life" are entirely different than those of any other person.

If you look around you, for example, you will recognise three or four people in your community who are about the same age, but each person, may have an entirely different lifestyle from the others. One person could be living alone; another married with four children; another divorced with two children; the last, married with no child.

The point I wish to make here is that comparing yourself with somebody else based on what you see will not really encourage you to fulfil your destiny. Instead, discovering your purpose in life will more surely get you to your destination. From the above example, the one who is living alone should not be judged as a failure because due to her circumstances she might have the time needed to achieve (academically, for example) more than the one who is married with four children.

The season for choosing a career, for the single person described above, might even last until she grows old. However, her achievements, and the legacy she might pass on to the next generation, could be far greater than the individual who gave birth to four children.

The Bible helps us to understand that although you might find many people doing the same job, or providing a particular service, if your purpose in life is to achieve that very same goal, (because you have been gifted by God) your achievement and your presentation will be so impressive and so uniquely done that great people will overlook the others and seek you out. This means there may be one particular thing in life that only you can do and the rest of creation is waiting for you to take your rightful place in destiny.

"A person's gift makes room for her and brings her before great people". [Proverbs 18:16-17]

TIPS

1. To pursue your dreams and creativity is what will bring you success in life.
2. Your uniqueness is a passport to your break through.
3. Great achievers in life are those who are willing to utilise their potential to cultivate something extraordinary from the ordinary.
4. Your fingerprints are different from every other person so don't walk in the shadow of others [be your own self]. Concentrate on what you are good at.
5. Never be discouraged if others don't share in your vision. The side on which you are standing determines the colour of a fence or a wall.
6. The way you perceive things in life is based on your make–up as a person, so to get others to understand your views you need to learn to express them.

PRIORITISING YOUR TIME

Prioritising available time is important if the virtuous woman is to realise her potential and achieve her God-given goals. The reason being, you cannot afford to be "Jack of all trades and master of none". You have not been created to solve the whole world's problems, as well as your own. You have only been designed as *part* of a *solution*, so find out what your part is and play it well. Whatever you do, have the Bible as your foundation. Find out through prayer and reading of the word of God whether it's in the plan (and purpose) God has for your life.

TIPS

1. Time, as some people say, is precious. Utilise your time wisely.
2. Time waits for nobody so never postpone what you can do today.
3. There is time for everything so do the right thing, at the right time.
4. Time has a way of revealing what has been done in the past so always plan ahead in whichever project you are engaged.
5. Time has a way of teaching us vital lessons so learn from your past experiences and also from others who are willing to share their experiences with you.
6. There are some issues that are worth leaving for time to solve. Time has a way of "telling" or making important decisions sometimes for us.

Because of the uniqueness of each individual, part of the service you will render towards the solution of problems will not benefit everyone. As a virtuous woman, be sensible; do what you can; be grateful for those who have been assigned to assist you; but do not make the mistake of dragging everybody along your path.

The Bible gives a good example using two sisters, Martha and Mary, who had an encounter with Jesus in their home.

Martha and Mary

"As Jesus and his disciples were on their way, he came to a village where a woman named Martha opened her home to him. She had a sister called Mary, who sat at the Lord's feet

listening to what he said. But Martha was distracted by all the preparations that had to be made. She came to him and asked, "Lord, don't you care that my sister has left me to do the work by myself? Tell her to help me!"

"Martha, Martha," the Lord answered, "you are worried and upset about many things, but only one thing is needed. Mary has chosen what is better, and it will not be taken away from her." [Luke 10:38-42]

Jesus did not rebuke Mary. That which Martha had said was not true, but more importantly He was trying to encourage Martha to stop being a busybody; to stop being hospitable to everyone and to make time to find out who she was and what she has been destined for in life. There is more to Christianity than the rendering of good services and that should not be (mistakenly) used as a substitute. Christianity is having a personal relationship with the Almighty God, The One who created the heaven and earth so that you can discover His plan and purpose for your life on this planet. The Bible describes this idea as follows: -

"*Not because of works, lest anyone should boast.* [It is not the result of what anyone can possibly do, so no one can boast of it].

For we are God's handiwork, His workmanship, recreated in Christ Jesus, [born anew] *that we, may do those good works, which God predestined and planned beforehand for us* [taking paths which He prepared ahead of time], *that we should walk in them*" [living the good life which He prearranged and made ready for us to live]. *[Ephesians 2:9-10]*

TIPS

1. Tell yourself, you have the choice and the ability to say, "no" instead of complaining. The Bible says, "God rewards a cheerful giver" not a complainer and those who give grudgingly. "*Every man according as he purposed in his heart, so let him give; not grudgingly, or of necessity: for God loved a cheerful giver. And God is able to make all grace abound toward you; that ye, always having all sufficiency in all things, may abound to every good work*". *[2 Corinthians 9: 8] KJV*
2. Whatever you want others to do for you, take the initiative and do it for them. The Bible says, "*Give, and it will be given to you. A good measure, pressed down, shaken together and running over, will be poured into your lap. For with the measure you use, it will be measured to you*". *[Luke 6:38]*
3. If you need a friend, you have to show yourself to be friendly. There is a saying, "Respect is earned not commanded".
4. Don't give out of a selfish motive or a hidden agenda. The recipient will be worse off if they discover the reasons behind your generosity.
5. Responsibilities in life are personal. What is personal to you might not be another person's "cup of tea".
6. Make it a point to show kindness to people because it is very rewarding and costs absolutely nothing in most cases.

TAKE RESPONSIBILITIES FOR YOUR ACTIONS

Each individual is responsible for leading a noble and God-fearing life. As such never allow others to run your life for you if you want to acquire happiness.

There is a saying, "Shine in the corner wherever you are". It is not everybody who will achieve such greatness and success like Bill Gates (of Microsoft), but a cleaner can work hard to obtain a cleaning company of her own.

Every human being has a gift and a talent from above. Identifying yours will give you a degree of success in your own field.

The questions you need to ask yourself are "Have I acquired enough wisdom to see me through my next stage in life"? "Who is my coach"? "Where am I getting my lessons and inspirations from"? "What manuals am I using"? "On whose theory is it based "?

Finally, am I going to cross-check my references or wait for the result of my actions first! Remember, there might not be the opportunity or time for correction as you are travelling, and are not stationed at the same place. Also remember, you are created to fulfil a specific purpose and if you fail on your mission, it will not be easy to replace you. As a result, you could be letting the whole of creation down.

THINGS TO REMEMBER

- Understanding your uniqueness will assist you to appreciate your place as a valuable team member [in your home, church community and in the world.]

- Knowing who you are in Christ Jesus will help you to understand your seasons in life. This will also help you to prioritise your time.
- There is one thing in life that only you can do best – discover what it is. Through prayer and by reading the Bible, devote all your heart and all your energy towards it.
- Life is channelled by your daily choices and sacrifices.
- Not everybody in life will celebrate you, but you could be the hero somebody is waiting for.
- To get a good counsel in life, you need somebody who has passed through similar difficulties: that means not every message you hear is directly relevant to your needs.
- There is a time and a place for everything so take full control of your life, because nobody knows you better than yourself.
- It is better to pursue a dream than to sit there doing nothing. "There is no harm in trying". At least if you fail, you will know where you went wrong.
- Assisting others to fulfil their dreams and visions in life is important but don't let anything stop you from pursuing yours when the time is right.
- Don't have a slavery mentality. Have a winning positive attitude in life and let everything you do be geared towards interpreting dreams of others as well as your own.
- Nobody in life is perfect so never feel ashamed or intimidated if you need to retrieve your steps to recover something you left behind.

- Listen to your critics but never allow them to feel there is any truth in what they are saying. In that way you can easily amend your ways and put them out of business completely.

Chapter Three

21ST CENTURY WOMAN WHO DOES NOT BELIEVE IN GOD
21ST CENTURY SINGLE WOMAN WHO DOES NOT BELIEVE IN GOD
21ST CENTURY MARRIED WOMAN WHO DOES NOT BELIEVE IN GOD
WOMEN AND WISDOM
DO NOT WORRY
THE HYMN OF A GOOD WOMAN

THE 21ST CENTURY WOMAN (who does not believe in God)

The 21st century woman without God sees herself as very wise and very smart but then didn't the Bible warn us that "*stupid people always think they are wise" [Proverbs 12:15] and that "Even if you beat fools until they are half dead, you still can't beat the foolishness out of them?"[Proverbs 27:22]*

The woman who thinks [in her heart] that there is no God, thinks of herself more highly than she ought to. She sometimes says to herself, "21st century woman, just what exactly does that mean"? After much thought, sometimes over a glass of wine, she says to herself, "Oh, yes. It means I am to eat as little food as possible and stay as thin as a walking stick. It means I am allowed to make my own living and pay my half when on a date with a man—after all, we live in an equal-rights society with men. It means I am allowed, not only to buy the condoms but also, to insist they are worn. It means, if the condom breaks, I should not expect this one-night stand or blind date to assist me to raise a child. After all, the encounter was meant for pleasure and pleasure alone. Best of all it means, I am allowed to have chains of emotionally handicapped men who can't commit, who want fun but have a fear of intimacy".

21st century woman, who does not believe in God sometimes says to herself, "When the going gets tough and I have no one to blame but myself, I am allowed to use my credit card to pay someone who make predictions—using demonic powers to tell me what the future holds".

The 21st century woman without God is worthless and, sad to say, lost—regardless of her materialistic and physical achievements. Deep down in her heart, if she is honest enough to admit it, there is this feeling of emptiness. Unfortunately she is heading for spiritual destruction. What does the Bible say about the 21st century single woman who does not believe in God?

"The woman Folly is loud; she is undisciplined and without knowledge. She sits at the door of her house, on a seat at the highest point of the city, calling out to those who pass by, who go straight on their way. "*Let all who are simple come in here!" she says to those who lack judgement.*

"Stolen water is sweet; food eaten in secret is delicious!" But little do they know that the dead are there, that her guests are in the depths of the grave". [Proverbs 9: 13-18]

TIPS

1 Wrongdoing is always appealing, but the consequence of that action needs to be investigated. This will help you to make up your mind if it is really worth it.

2. In life and destiny, you portray how others treat you. Your approach should always be from a positive perspective or else you give others the choice to treat you any way they wish.
3. It is good to have fun, but make a point to be conscious enough to determine whether the place in which you are sleeping is safe.
4. It is sad when people say, "If only I had known" or when they have a regret in life. As the saying goes, "Prevention is better than cure." Protect yourself because you only live once.
5. Make it your responsibility to be spiritually sound so that you can discern what is good and evil.

6. "Show me your friend, and I will tell you your character." This is just a saying but the truth is that any close acquaintances you have either add value to your life or deduct from it.

The 21st century married woman who does not acknowledge God is equally naive. She believes the way to bring some sanity into her confused world is to seek love outside of her marriage and to wipe her face like a sweet innocent girl when her husband is around. She says to herself' "Those husbands are emotionally handicapped, despite being married all these years and having children. If they are still afraid of intimacy, I need to do something with my life before I become emotionally crippled as well."

She calls her husband "Darling" but behind his back she is more deadly than a poisonous snake. What does the Bible also say about 21st century married woman who does not believe in God?

"At the window of my house I looked out through the lattice.

I saw among the simple, I noticed among the young men, a youth who lacked judgement. He was going down the street near her corner, walking along in the direction of her house at twilight, as the day was fading, as the dark of night set in. Then out came a woman to meet him, dressed like a prostitute and with crafty intent. (She is loud and defiant; her feet never stay at home; now in the street, now in the squares, at every corner she lurks.) She took hold of him and kissed him and with a brazen face she said: "I have fellowship offerings at home; today I fulfilled my vows. So I came out to meet you; I looked for you and have found you! I have covered my bed with coloured linens from Egypt. I have perfumed my bed with myrrh, aloes and cinnamon. Come, let's drink deep of love till morning; let's enjoy ourselves with love! My husband is not at home; he has gone on a long journey. He took his purse filled with money and will not be home till full moon." With persuasive words she led him astray; she seduced him with her smooth talk. All at once he followed her like an ox going to the slaughter, like a deer stepping into a noose 'til an arrow

pierces his liver, like a bird darting into a snare, little knowing it will cost him his life. Now then, my son, listen to me; pay attention to what I say. Do not let your heart turn to her ways or stray into her paths. Many are the victims she has brought down; her slain are a mighty throng. Her house is a highway to the grave, leading down to the chambers of death".
[Proverbs 7:6- 27]

The word of God describes such a woman as dangerous. Such a woman is never pleased nor satisfied about anything, and her soul, if not brought under the submission of the Almighty God, is like a wild fire consuming and destroying anything she comes into contact with including her home.

The sad story is that most children who get entangled with marital problems of their parents do so through no fault of their own, and they suffer the consequences. The Bible says:

"*Every wise woman builds her house but the foolish pluck it down with her hands." [Proverbs 14:1]*

Many marriages and relationships are in a mess due to the fact that the woman has refused to put her trust and confidence in God. Having done so, she has chosen to follow the dictates of her mind instead of the counsel and guidance of the Holy Spirit.

The Bible tells us, "*The fear of the LORD is the beginning of wisdom; all who follow his precepts have good understanding. To him belongs eternal praise. [Psalm 111:10]*

TIPS

1. There is a saying, "The evil which men do, lives after them". Try not to sow seeds that will come and hunt you in the future.
2. Keeping secrets in life will keep you going for a while, but never bank your life on it because secrets always have a way of unfolding when least expected.
3. "It takes two to tango", but sometimes do a self-assessment: it will surprise you to discover that "pointing accusing finger at somebody always leaves the remaining four facing your direction."
4. Children are a gift and if one desires peace in old age then do what it takes to nurture them properly, so that they can at least cater for themselves when they are old.
5. Investing in another person is the most rewarding project you can ever embark on. Even if the person cannot pay you back, rest assured you will never lose your reward.
6. In life and destiny the same people you meet when climbing up will be exactly the same ones you will meet on your way down, so never take people for granted.

WOMAN ANDWISDOM

"By wisdom a house is built, and through understanding it is established; through knowledge its rooms are filled with rare and beautiful treasures. A wise woman has great power, and a woman of knowledge increases strength; for waging war you need guidance, and for victory, many advisers".[Proverbs 24:3-6]

The virtuous woman, from a biblical point of view, is meant to be smarter, more responsible and more sensible than the ordinary woman of the 21st century described above. Although each day presents her with fresh challenges, the Lord Jesus Christ guides and empowers her to meet each trial with a cool head and a good heart; with His help she will not succumb to temptation.

Seeking the Lord gives the woman focus and an anchor for her soul. It strengthens her will and gives her the sanity to be in control even when all things around her are falling apart. Knowing that there is always that "Rock" (which is above her earthly limitations) for her to rely on when her heart grows faint is a great source of comfort for the virtuous woman.

There are words in the Bible, which have so much life and power in them that they are stronger than any therapy.

Without the teachings of the Word of God and the daily guidance of the Holy Spirit, the woman is often not strong enough to overcome the constant worry in the battlefield of her mind. She worries about her finances, about her bills, about her children and about her husband. She worries about how she looks and in most cases, finds herself being drawn back into old habits and patterns of worrying, even if there is nothing to be concerned about.

God The Creator neither wants the woman to be tormented with worries, nor to be anxious about things she needs in life. For He has already made provision for them in His covenant and what, the woman has to do is to seek Him through His word and follow the plan and purpose ordained for her life.

Constant worry is a torment and the word of God agrees:

"A merry heart does good like a medicine, but a crushed spirit dries up the bones." [Proverbs 17:22]

A positive attitude will bring you more favour and co-operation than a negative one. When you keep adding to the heat and confusion of a crisis, people lose faith in your ability to handle things under pressure; but if you keep cool and maintain your sense of humour when things are falling apart, they will show their appreciation.

"God has not given us the spirit of fear but He has given unto us a Spirit of Power of Love and of a Sound Mind [Self Control]." *[2 Timothy 1:7]*

TIPS

1. If you are in need of somebody's assistance, wearing a cheerful smile on your face might attract somebody looking your direction.
2. A sad countenance is like building a wall around you, but what you need to discover is that there are many more people facing exactly the same challenges as you, yet getting on with their lives.
3. Happiness is by choice: remember, it is contagious just like sadness.
4. Never allow another human being to determine or set your moods in life. You never know when they will start playing with your emotions.

5. The Bible says, " *Keep your heart with all diligence, for out of it spring the issues of life*". *[Proverbs 4:23]* In life make sure you have your [own little] space because deep down in your heart there is space for only one [and that is for The Creator]. No other person is worthy enough to occupy that space.
6. Mankind is like clay in the potter's hands. Finding out what the maker is moulding you to be, will give you rest. Besides the potter's decision of how the clay turns out is unquestionable.

DO NOT WORRY

"Therefore I tell you, do not worry about your life, what you will eat or drink; or about your body, what you will wear. Is not life more important than food, and the body more important than clothes? Look at the birds of the air; they do not sow or reap or store away in barns, and yet your heavenly Father feeds them. Are you not much more valuable than they? Who of you by worrying can add a single hour to his life?" And why do you worry about clothes? See how the lilies of the field grow. They do not labour or spin. Yet I tell you that not even Solomon in all his splendour was dressed like one of these. If that is how God clothes the grass of the field, which is here today and tomorrow is thrown into the fire, will he not much more clothe you, O you of little faith? So do not worry, saying, 'What shall we eat?' or 'What shall we drink?' or 'What shall we wear?' For the pagans run after all these things, and your heavenly Father knows that you need them. But seek first his kingdom and his righteousness, and all these things will be given to you as well. Therefore do not worry about tomorrow, for tomorrow will worry about itself. Each day has enough trouble of it's own". [Matthew 6:25-34]

Virtuous woman, The Creator wants you to understand that, "*The fear of the Lord, is the beginning of Wisdom; all who follow his precepts have good understanding*".

[Proverbs 1:7]

Any other fear pertaining to your daily needs to survive on this earth is a torment from the devil; such fear, if not brought under the subjection of the Spirit of God, can bring destruction to your soul.

TIPS

1. There is an escape route in any given situation. Instead of being fearful, pray for God to show you the way out. Also seek for professional assistance; remember somebody has already been through the challenges you are facing.
2. Fear is a torment. Instead of it stopping you from having a good night's sleep, find something positive to meditate on.
3. The righteous, as the Bible says, are "as bold as a lion". "*The wicked man flees though no one pursues, but the righteous are as bold as a lion*".*[Proverbs 28:1]*

   Instead of talking about your fears to magnify it, tell yourself you are more than a conqueror, and boast in what God can do about your situation.
4. Fear, if not overcome, can lead you into sin. The Bible says, "*Do not boast about tomorrow, for you do not know what a day may bring forth*". *[Proverbs 27:1]*

   Don't allow what you are fearful of today determines your decisions for the future.

5. There are different types of fear, but in most cases they are all in the mind. Trusting your Creator to see you through difficult times will provide a platform for you to stand on.
6. Always look for positive words to combat your fear.

The woman who is being tormented in her mind with worry and anxiety about materialistic things in life is such a dangerous and difficult person to live with. She is self-centred, and never satisfied. She thinks being financially secure or being able to climb on top of "the social ladder", (through academic achievements or having a successful business) will fill the vacuum in her soul, but that has been proved to be false.

Virtuous woman, if the above describes the situation you are in, remember it is never too late to change your ways. Stop where you are right now and renew the relationship between you and God, your Creator, The Maker of heaven and earth.

Say the following sinner's prayers aloud: -

"Dear God, I am a sinner, I do not even deserve to pray to you; but I understand that it does not matter where I am coming from.

I understand that what I have nor have not done in the past does not matter. I understand I can pray to you, right now, through your dear son, Jesus Christ who died at The Calvary Cross and you will wipe away my past and forgive me my sins.

Please forgive me, in the name of Jesus and make me your child once again. Father God, please fill me with Your Holy

Spirit and make me strong so that I do not go back to my old ways again.

In Jesus' Mighty Name I pray, Amen".

THINGS TO REMEMBER

* If you have prayed the sinner's prayers, the next thing is for you to pray daily to Father God through His dear Son, Jesus Christ.
* Secondly, get yourself a Bible and begin to read it daily, praying to Father God to assist you by His Holy Spirit to understand what you read.
* The next thing is for you to join a church where Jesus Christ is being preached. If you cannot find a church to join, find yourself a study partner and study the Bible together.
* Use the words you read in the Bible to build yourself up.

For example, say to yourself daily: -

"Father God has not given me the Spirit of fear and anxiety. *He has given unto me, The Spirit of Power,*

The Spirit of Love, and a Sound Mind". [2 Timothy 1:7]

To be a virtuous woman, or a woman of noble character, should be the aim and focus for every woman. The Bible describes such a woman as "valuable" and "wise".

THE HYMN TO A GOOD WOMAN

A wife of noble character who can find? She is worth far more than rubies.

Her husband has full confidence in her and lacks nothing of value. She brings him good, not harm, all the days of her life. She selects wool and flax and works with eager hands. She is like the merchant ships, bringing her food from afar. She gets up while it is still dark; she provides food for her family and portions for her servant girls.

She considers a field and buys it; out of her earnings she plants a vineyard. She sets about her work vigorously; her arms are strong for her tasks. She sees that her trading is profitable, and her lamp does not go out at night. In her hand she holds the distaff and grasps the spindle with her fingers. She opens her arms to the poor and extends her hands to the needy. When it snows, she has no fear for her household; for all of them are clothed in scarlet. She makes coverings for her bed; she is clothed in fine linen and purple.

Her husband is respected at the city gate, where he takes his seat among the elders of the land. She makes linen garments and sells them, and supplies the merchants with sashes. She is clothed with strength and dignity; she can laugh at the days to come.

She speaks with wisdom, and faithful instruction is on her tongue. She watches over the affairs of her household and does not eat the bread of idleness. Her children arise and call her blessed; her husband also, and he praises her: "Many women do noble things, but you surpass them all." Charm is deceptive, and beauty is fleeting; but a woman who fears the Lord is to be praised. Give her the reward she has earned, and let her works bring her praise at the city gate".

[Proverbs 31:10-31]

Chapter Four

UNDERSTANDING HUMAN BEINGS
GOD AND HUMAN SPIRIT
JESUS AND THE HUMAN SOUL
THE TEN COMMANDMENTS
THE HOLY SPIRIT AND HUMAN BODY

In order to have full control of her thoughts and to walk in the will and purpose of God, the virtuous woman will first have to find out about the functions of her body from God's creative point of view.

UNDERSTANDING HUMAN BEINGS

Before the woman can effectively deal with most situations in life, and walk in the plan and purpose, which God has for her, she has to first have full understanding of who she really is (both physically and spiritually). The woman is not simply flesh and bone, but she was fearfully and wonderfully made by her creator to perform many different functions. The human body (or being) comprises of three main parts according to the word of God. The Bible explains these parts as follows:—"*May the God of peace Himself sanctify you holy; and may your spirit, soul and body be kept sound and blameless at the coming of our Lord Jesus Christ". [1Thessalonians 5:23]*

HUMAN BODY ➡ HUMAN SOUL ➡ HUMAN SPIRIT

The human body or flesh, as shown above, is the outward cover for the human soul and spirit. When a person dies, the human body expires, but the soul and the human spirit still move on to either Heaven or Hell.

Therefore the woman is a three-in-one being, made in the image and likeness of God.

The three major components, which define human beings, can be compared with The Trinity.

God The Creator believes in 'Three-in-one' and this is what he had in mind when He said, in the book of Genesis, "Let us make mankind in our image". It can be said; He created the human spirit, soul and body, in the likeness of The Trinity.

"Let Us [Father, Son, and Holy Spirit] *make mankind in Our image, after Our likeness, and let them have complete authority over the fish of the sea, the birds of the air, the* [tame] *beasts, and over all of the earth, and over everything that creeps upon the earth". [Genesis 1:26]*

The book of Ecclesiastes explains why three are better than one. "*Again, if two lie down together, then they have warmth; but how can one be warm alone? And though a man might prevail against him who is alone, two will withstand him. A threefold cord is not quickly broken". [Ecclesiastes 4:11-12]*

Human beings, who are made up of human spirit, soul and body, were created as the "Trinity" to represent a cord that cannot easily be broken. Just like 'Trinity', all three aspects of one's self have to be in harmony to achieve the best result possible, according to God's will.

A Song:

"Holy, Holy, Holy! Lord God Almighty
Early in the morning, our song shall rise to Thee:
Holy, Holy, Holy, merciful and might,
God in three Persons blessed Trinity".

The song, "God in Three Persons", gives us a clear understanding of how The Trinity works. The concept of Trinity, (God The Father, The Son (Jesus) and The Holy Spirit) goes a long way towards explaining the three aspects of one's self, namely spirit, soul and body. Each aspect of 'self' was created to represent, reflect and relate to each Personality in The Trinity. This can be illustrated as follows: -

The Human Spirit ⟺ GOD

The Human Soul ⟺ JESUS

The Human Body ⟺ THE HOLY SPIRIT

GOD AND HUMAN SPIRIT

The spirit of mankind was created to relate directly to God. Though human beings live on earth, they are meant to be in constant communion with God, through the human spirit.

God and the human spirit

"Yet a time is coming and has now come, when the true worshipers will worship the Father in spirit and truth, for they are the kind of worshippers the Father seeks. God is spirit, and His worshippers must worship Him in spirit and in truth." [John 4:22-23]

To be a worshipper, or to be in constant communion with God, is simply to acknowledge God at all times of the day, thanking and praising Him as you go about your daily activities. It takes a lot of practice, but as you do it more often "He" becomes your "invisible Father", whom you alone can feel at all times. As the relationship between you and God intensifies, an inner awareness of His continual presence is developed.

JESUS AND THE HUMAN SOUL

Jesus' mission on earth was to assist the human soul to make the right choices that will pave the way for the human spirit to relate to God. Jesus did this by simplifying the Ten Commandments and showing mankind how to find, and follow, the narrow road that leads to the Kingdom of God.

Jesus and the human soul

Then one of them who was a Lawyer, ask him a question, tempting him, and saying;
Teacher, which kind of commandment is great and important in the Law? And He replied to him, You shall, love the Lord your God with all your heart and with all your soul and with your entire mind). This is the greatest and the most important commandment: The second most important commandment is to love your neighbour as yourself." [Matthew 22:36-38]

The commandments, as given to Moses in the book of Exodus, were difficult for the human mind (soul) to comprehend, so Jesus came to simplify them. The Ten Commandments as given to Moses are as follows: -

"And God spoke all these words: I am the Lord your God, who brought you out of Egypt, out of the land of slavery. You shall have no other gods before me. You shall not make for yourself an idol in the form of anything in heaven above or on the earth beneath or in the waters below. You shall not bow down to them or worship them; for I, the Lord your God, am a jealous God, punishing the children for the sin of the fathers to the third and fourth generation of those who hate me, but showing love to a thousand [generations] of those who love me and keep my commandments. You shall not misuse the name of the Lord your God, for the Lord will not hold anyone guiltless who misuses his name. Remember the Sabbath day by keeping it holy. Six days you shall labour and do all your work, but the seventh day is a Sabbath to the Lord your God. On it you shall not do any work, neither you, nor your son or daughter, nor your manservant or maidservant, nor your animals, nor the alien within your gates. For in six days the LORD made the heavens and the earth, the sea, and all that is in them, but he rested on the seventh day. Therefore the Lord blessed the Sabbath day and made it holy. Honour your father and your mother, so that you may live long in the land the Lord your God is giving you.

You shall not murder.

You shall not commit adultery.

You shall not steal.

You shall not give false testimony against your neighbour.

You shall not covet your neighbour's house. You shall not covet your neighbour's wife, or his manservant or maidservant, his ox or donkey, or anything that belongs to *your neighbour. [Exodus 20: 1-17]*

TIPS

1. Rules, regulations and policies in life are there as a measure of precaution. Once you understand the reasons why they are being enforced, and their advantages, you will embrace them with joy.
2. There are certain rules in life that are not for negotiation. Breaking such rules is detrimental to your well-being, so invest time to find out what they are in any society in which you find yourself.
3. Reading the book of Proverbs in the Bible will give you Insight into spiritual rules that cannot be tampered with. "*The fear of the LORD is the beginning of knowledge, but fools despise wisdom and discipline*". *[Proverbs 1:7]*. This will help you to find out certain spiritual laws, which need to be observed with care.
4. Certain rules made by family members and those in authority can be set in place out of their own selfish motives. To free yourself from such rules, prayer, wisdom and meekness are required to make your views known.

5 The Bible states that, we should give honour, to whom honour is due. Sometimes the people whom we should respect don't even deserve it, but for the sake of peace, show your respect anyway. Leave it for the conscience of that person to do the judgement.

6. When it comes to dealing with people, always take the "peace option". It might even make you look stupid initially, but don't worry. You will be the hero in the end "*Blessed are the peacemakers, for they will be called sons of God*". [*Matthew* 5:9]

Fulfilling The Ten Commandments with Love

Jesus' mission on earth was to encourage the soul of mankind to resist evil and to accept the correct way of life. He achieved this by summarising the Ten Commandments into three statements:

Love the Lord your God with all your heart and with all your soul and with your whole mind. Love your neighbour as you love yourself, [Matthew 22:36-38] representing once again, a "*cord that cannot easily be broken*". This can be demonstrated as follows:

"*God in Three Persons*", who created mankind to be "three-in-one" in His image, knows that if human beings relate to each other with love (God's love) that relationship will represent the **"*threefold cord,*** *which is not easily broken*". *[Ecclesiastes 4:11-12]*

This means that if human beings relate to each other in a similar way, namely the way God sees mankind (as spiritual beings, perfect and flawless), that relationship will be strong enough to withstand any test. This is why

Jesus said; "If somebody offends you seventy times seven times in a day, still forgive the person".

"Then Peter came to Jesus and asked, "Lord, how many times shall I forgive my brother when he sins against me? Up to seven times?" Jesus answered, "I tell you, not seven times, but seventy times seven times". *[Matthew 18: 21-22]*

According to the Old Testament, The Ten Commandments were impossible for human beings to follow, so when Jesus came, he simplified them and made them more meaningful. He told us that what we have to remember, are these three things as follows: -

- **Love your God [with all heart, soul and mind].**
- **Love your neighbour [as yourself].**
- **Love your own self [as your neighbour].**

With the above statement Jesus was trying to get mankind to think about God in three Persons, the three aspects of 'self' and how we should relate with one another.

Jesus said; "Do not think that I have come to do away with or undo the Law or the Prophets; I have come not to do away with or undo but to complete and fulfil them. For truly I tell you, until the sky and earth pass away and perish, not one smallest letter nor one little hook [identifying certain Hebrew letters] *will pass from the Law until all things are accomplished.*

Whoever then breaks or does away with or relaxes one of the least important of these commandments and teaches others to do so shall be called least important in the kingdom of heaven, but he who practices them and teaches others to do so shall be called great in the kingdom of heaven.

For I tell you, unless your righteousness (your morality and virtue) *is more than that of the Scribes and Pharisees, you will never enter the kingdom of heaven".* [*Matthew 5:17-20*]

Reading the Bible will help you to see that God was aware of the difficulties the human soul would encounter on Earth. That is the reason why He sent Jesus to show us the way.

THE LAW OF MOSES MADE SIMPLER

If you love God, your neighbour and yourself, this love will sustain that friendship in perfect unity. Can you imagine how the world would be like, if we all walked on this Earth representing and reflecting The Trinity in perfect love with one another?

"So in everything, do to others what you would have them do to you, for this sums up the Law and the Prophets". [Matthew 7:12]

TWELVE GOLDEN RULES FOR LOVE

Love is patient
Love is kind
Love does not envy
Love does not boast
Love is not proud
Love is not rude
Love is not self-seeking
Love is not easily angered
Love does not keep records of wrong
Love does not delight in evil but rejoices with truth
Love, protects, trust, hopes and perseveres.
Love never fails.

Exhibiting the above characteristics will get you past every barrier in life. Love is commonly known as a feeling, but God's love [Agape love] is not just a feeling but also a powerful tool to bring harmony when relating with others.

Exhibiting love is useful not only in relating to members of your family but it is a secret weapon to use in your relationship with those who even hate and despise you. When you exhibit the above characteristics of love no harm can ever come near you because you will be walking with the shield of the Creator Himself around you. Every human being on earth responds to this kind of love because it is a need that has been created deep in human soul to be fulfilled. Remember, as hard as another human being might try to fulfil this craving in our souls, it is only The Creator who can fully satisfy us with His Agape Love.

TIPS

1. If a relationship is worth fighting for, and you have tried every other method, try gaining insight of how to love unconditionally with the Agape Love. It's a device everyone responds to.
2. Agape Love will keep you in perfect peace because while others are thinking of how to get rid of somebody, you will be thinking of how to help the same person to overcome their shortcomings, which in actual fact could be to your advantage.
3. Believing in the dreams of people close to you sometimes helps you to also accomplish your own dreams. Nobody in life achieves success alone. Somewhere along the line everybody needs assistance from somebody.
4. Love knows no boundaries so any time you are being protective of what you have, ask yourself if you are really walking in God's kind of love. You cannot respond to the needs of everyone, but those who are in your inner circle in life [close relatives and some acquaintances] are there for a purpose.
5. Any time you keep bringing up past unpleasant experiences, tell yourself you are falling out of love because love keeps no record of wrong.
6. True love is unconditional. The other person doesn't even have to exhibit the same qualities to earn it.

THE HOLY SPIRIT AND THE HUMAN BODY

The Holy Spirit came to empower women to do the work for which they are destined. The Holy Spirit reveals to the woman who she really is, in Christ Jesus (in His covenant).

THE HOLY SPIRIT AND THE HUMAN BODY

Do you not know that your body is the temple [the very sanctuary] of the Holy Spirit who lives within you, whom you have received [as a Gift] from God? You are not your own. You were bought at a price [made His own by the death of Jesus]. So then, honour God and bring glory to Him in your body. [1 Corinthians 6:19-20]

If the virtuous woman understands the teachings of Jesus (regarding who she really is in Christ, and the power, made available to her through the Holy Spirit), she will be careful in regard to those things with which she brings her body into contact.

For example, if the virtuous woman loves herself and understands that The Holy Spirit dwells in her, she will immediately refrain from anything that will pollute her body, e.g. adultery, fornication, smoking and excessive drinking of alcohol.

Just as the Trinity works together in unity and harmony, so also the three aspects of self interact. Each has a function but no one function is greater than another, nor does any function actually precede another. All are interrelated in an exactly equal way and should work together in harmony to achieve the optimum results, as ordained by the Creator. A tired body is of no use to neither the human soul nor spirit. The soul that is not sound cannot co-operate with either the human spirit or body. Also, the spirit,which is not in communion with God, cannot direct the soul and body to achieve the purpose God has for the individual.

In order to function properly as an individual, each of the three aspects of oneself should be in good health and at peace with one another.

Chapter Five

HUMAN BEINGS
THE HUMAN BODY
THE HUMAN SOUL
RENEWING OF THE MIND
UN—FORGIVENESS
THE NEW PLAN

CREATION (GOD'S ORIGINAL PLAN)

And God said, "Let the land produce living creatures according to their kinds: livestock, creatures that move along the ground, and wild animals, each according to its kind." And it was so. God made the wild animals according to their kinds, the livestock according to their kinds, and all the creatures that move along the ground according to their kinds. And God saw that it was good.

Then God said, "Let us make man in our image, in our likeness, and let them rule over the fish of the sea and the birds of the air, over the livestock, over all the earth, and over all the creatures that move along the ground." So God created man in his own image, in the image of God he created him; male and female he created them.

[Genesis 1: 24-27]

To be able to understand God's plan and purpose for the virtuous woman, let us look carefully at human beings and analyse each function of the human self (body, soul and spirit), moving from the known (the human body on earth) to the unknown (where the human spirit dwells.)

THE HUMAN BODY- (Body, Soul and Spirit)

THE BODY	SOUL	HUMAN SPIRIT
Flesh	Will	Conscience
Outward Sheath	Mind / Emotions	Commune

THE HUMAN BODY

The body, which is described in the dictionary as the entire physical structure of human beings, was formed out of the dust of the ground according to the book of Genesis. This clearly defines the origin of the first people ever to live on Earth [Adam and Eve]. God specifically created the human body for use whilst on Earth (earth bound). He gave mankind dominion over all other things i.e. the fowl of the air, the fish of the sea, cattle and every creeping thing that creeps upon the earth.

THE HUMAN SOUL

The soul conceives ideas, the mind develops these ideas and once a thought or idea is born the body experiences it.

The soul is described as the immaterial part of a human being and is regarded as immortal.

The moral and intellectual values of a person are formed here. The soul is what constitutes the personality of each individual. There are three main functions to the soul, namely: will, mind and emotions.

The woman makes decisions and choices of her own free will and that is why each person's wants, needs, likes and dislikes vary from others. The soul of a person has the ability of influencing her will, to choose and express her agreement (or not) on an issue. This freedom of choice is even recognised by God, and that is the main reason why it is an individual's choice whether or not to accept and recognise God. Without it, a person is reduced to being an automaton.

The Spirit of God can only assist and give comfort to a person who, out of her own free will, has made the initial quality decision to choose God's way, through His Son Jesus rather than the dictates of the mind and the evil thoughts presented daily by Satan and his agents.

The mind of a person is the instrument, which forms our thoughts. It manifests our intellectual power. Out of it comes wisdom, knowledge, and reasoning. It is what makes a person sane.

Emotion is the faculty of our likes and dislikes. Through it we are able to express the whole spectrum of emotions such as love, hate, sadness and happiness.

A person's soul is just as easily influenced by past experiences as it is by environment. Once a person's soul is firmly established in a concept, it takes considerable effort for that person to change. This is the main reason why it is difficult for somebody to modify bad habits.

This is why the Bible constantly reminds us to renew our mind or our commitment to God.

RENEWING OF THE MIND

Because the human mind is influenced by past experience as well as environment, the woman cannot instantly change her bad ways as soon as she becomes a Christian. First and foremost she has to understand the reason behind the need for that change. Secondly, she has to show her willingness to make that change. Finally, with the positive word of God, she must counteract any negative thoughts she has had.

For example, a child who was sexually abused will grow up carrying resentment, fear and anger throughout her whole life. This experience may even prevent her from getting married. For such a person to change her preconceived ideas about men, she needs to understand that not all men abuse children sexually. If married, she needs to understand that her marriage could end in divorce if she cannot come to terms with her experiences. She will then have to be willing to release her abuser from her thoughts, by forgiving him. Lastly, the empty space she has just created in her mind by forgiving him will need to be filled with the promises of God, by repeating to herself Bible quotations such as, "*I can do all things through Christ who strengthens me*"; "*Greater is He* [Jesus] *who is in me than he* [Satan] *that is in the world*" *[1John 4:3-4]*

TIPS

1. Never waste your whole life harbouring ill feelings towards others. They might not even be aware of your feelings, whilst rather enjoying their lives.
2. Hate can totally destroy you, so if you value your life then find ways of resolving issues.

3. Unresolved issues can prevent you from interacting with people who, in one way or another, might have assisted you in life.
4. Unresolved issues destroy homes, families and even nations, so act quickly whilst you have the chance.
5. 'Building a hedge' around yourself because you have once been hurt will not solve any problem. Rather, it will prevent you from leading a fulfilled life.
6. Human beings have different temperament. Not taking them seriously will help you get along with most of them.

Renewing your mind.

"Do not conform any longer to the pattern of this world, but be transformed by the renewing of your mind. Then you will be able to test and approve what God's will is. His good, pleasing and perfect will." [Romans 12:2]

THE HUMAN MIND AND EMOTIONS
THE UNRENEWED MIND

PAST SITUATIONS ➜ **EMOTIONS** ⬅ THE MIND

The mind that is not renewed by the Word of God reflects nothing other than previous bad emotional experiences; this mind is trapped. Any time such a person wants to move on; to create new concepts and ideas, the mind becomes like a recorded tape, which has been looped. The mind constantly replays only the bad things.

These experiences then become emotional strongholds, which take over the person's ability to reason.

The human mind plays a vital role in how we relate and respond to issues of life. The renewing of one's mind to reflect on God's wisdom gives different perspectives of ways in which to deal with issues. It enables individuals not to be driven by selfish ambitions and fear, but rather it helps and encourages us to live life to the full. Every battle in life is first overcome in the mind. The body is just there to convey the success of that battle.

Diagram 1-The mind that is not renewed by the word of God

BAD EXPERENCES	EMOTIONS	MIND	PRESENT STATE OF THE PERSON
Bad experiences from: Childhood Marriage Sickness	Fear, frustration, anger, insecurity. Inability to love one's self or others. Bitterness, unhappiness.	The mind that is not renewed dwells on past experiences and is trapped in darkness	Disbelief in the word of God. Does not know God's will and purpose for her life

RENEWED MIND

PAST SITUATIONS➡EMOTIONS➡MIND➡WILL OF GOD

The mind that is renewed by the word of God has wiped off all the bad experiences of the past. All stored up negative emotions has been turned to strength and the person is ready to move on to do exploit and find out the reason for her existence.

Diagram 2- Renewed mind that is ready to serve God

BAD EXPERENCES	EMOTIONS	MIND	PRESENT STATE OF THE PERSON
Bad experiences from: Childhood Marriage Sickness	Negative emotions erased by reading and studying the word of God	The renewed mind accepts God and trust in His word. Able to accept the mysteries of God.	Believes in God and is ready to find out God's will and purpose for her life.

The word of God acts like an eraser in your mind. It wipes away all the bad memories and replaces them with the truths, such as confidence, assurance and the security we have in God. The Bible tells us that it is only after renewing our minds, can we count ourselves worthy to stand in His presence and receive the Holy Spirit.

UN—FORGIVENESS

The most difficult emotional scars to heal are usually hurts and wounds sustained from the careless actions or words of loved ones. The only way to let go of such pain is to act like Jesus, by making excuses for the other person's actions.

Making excuses for a person who has hurt you will create a tunnel or an escape route in your mind for the 'poisonous venom' of 'hurt to escape from your soul and your body. This 'poisonous venom' can be compared with that of a poisonous snake, which if not expelled from your system will ultimately cause physical illness that could even lead to death.

'Un-forgiveness', if not dealt with, will eventually act like soot in a chimney, blocking all ventilation. It will act the same way by blocking off your human spirit from its communion with God. In order for Jesus to have free access to the Father, He had to create an escape route from his soul, mind and body for the feelings of rejection, anger, torment and hurt by making excuses for his accusers.

"When they got to the place called Skull Hill, they crucified him [Jesus] *along with the criminals, one on his right and the other on his left. Jesus prayed, "***Father, forgive them; they don't know what they're doing."** *And they divided up his clothes by casting lots.*

The people stood watching, and the rulers even sneered at him. They said, "He saved others; let him save himself if he is the Christ of God, the Chosen One." [Luke 23:34-35]

If Jesus, the Son of God, was able to make excuses for the people who killed him, then for our own good it should not be too big a problem to follow his example.

Even if you know very well that the person who has hurt you fully intended to cause you that hurt, formulate an excuse for your own sake. By doing so, your mind will accept the person's actions and create a gateway to allow the 'venom', which such actions has injected into your system to escape. In doing this, you will have the strength to pray for the person, and permanently release him or her from your thoughts in peace. This action of liberation will eventually help you even to love those who have hurt you badly.

TIPS

1. Un-forgiveness is unhealthy and beside that, you can never control the actions of another person, so why not get on with your life positively?
2. By not forgiving, you are trying to make a statement, but the sad truth is that nobody will learn or receive any kind of advice from you if what you are offering is motivated by hate and resentment.
3. Un-forgiveness will lead you to make decisions you could regret for the rest of your life.
4. Forgiving somebody who has hurt you badly in life gives you a step ahead over that person. It helps you to channel your life and energy positively.
5. Always seek professional help if somebody has unlawfully attacked you, but never take the law into your own hands, because you might find yourself serving the same sentence for the other person.
6. No human being is perfect so forgive others if you wish for others to do the same for you.

THE HUMAN SPIRIT

The human spirit is the part that communes with a higher Being; with God. The spirit of the woman collects information from the Spirit of God, and passes it on to her soul to be acted upon by the body. The spirit, (or the breath) as stated in the Bible [Genesis 2:7] is what gives life to a person on Earth. The Bible says that "*God is a Spirit and they that* [out of their own free will] *worship Him must worship Him in spirit and in truth*". [*John 4: 23*] The Spiritual aspect of an individual is the only part that can commune with God.

The functions of the human spirit can be classified into three main categories, namely: Conscience, Intuition and Communion. The conscience of a human being is an internal mechanism that differentiates right from wrong, not through the influence of knowledge stored up in the mind but by spontaneous, direct judgement. The word of God describes this as foll**ows: -**

The NEW PLAN

It will not be like the covenant I made with their forefathers
when I took them by the hand to lead them out of Egypt,
because they did not remain faithful to my covenant,
and I turned away from them, declares the Lord.
This is the covenant I will make with the house of Israel
after that time, declares the Lord. I will put my laws in their minds
and write them on their hearts. I will be their God, and they will be my people. No longer will a man teach his neighbour, or a man his brother, saying, 'Know the Lord,'
because they will all know me,
from the least of them to the greatest. [Hebrews 8:9-11]

Intuition that comes from the spirit of a woman is the knowledge that comes to human beings without conscious thought. Sometimes, we know things through intuition, and the mind just assists us to understand. The revelations of God and all the movements of the Holy Spirit are known to us through intuition.

A Christian must heed two things, the voice of the conscience and the teachings of the Spirit of God (through intuitions).

We are also to commune daily with God—worshipping and giving the honour and adoration that are due to Him. According to the Bible, one of the main reasons why God created human beings was to have dominion over His creation and have communion with Him [God].

The personality of an individual dwells in the soul, whereas the five senses—feel, touch, smell, taste and hearing—dwell in the body. Human beings are then described as Spiritual Beings with a Soul, living in a Body. It is through the corporal body that 'human beings' come into contact with the material world. The soul belongs to 'a person' and the spirit, because it affords us our relationship with God, could be termed as God-consciousness.

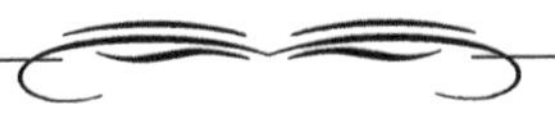

Chapter Six

PLAN OF SALVATION
JESUS THE LIGHT
PRAYER
THINGS TO REMEMBER

PLAN OF SALVATION

When 'human beings' sinned at the beginning (Genesis), God, by His infinite wisdom, devised a plan so that they would not perish on earth. This is known as the Plan of Salvation, which was carried out through His dear Son, Jesus Christ. Through Jesus, humanity can make its way back to where it originated (from God) and enjoy eternal life. Jesus came to show mankind how to live successfully on earth and to achieve life eternal through worship.

TIPS

1. Good works or being helpful to others is wonderful but the Bible has made it clear that, "works alone" is not a passport for entering into 'The Kingdom of God' or life eternal. The key is believing that Jesus is the Son of God. "*For God so loved the world that he gave his one and only Son, that whoever*

believes in him shall not perish but have eternal life. [John 3:16]

2. Rather, salvation or being 'saved' will reveal the good works God has predestined you to perform. "*Not by works, so that no one can boast. For we are God's workmanship, created in Christ Jesus to do good works, which God prepared in advance for us to do, in Christ". [Ephesians 2:9-10]*
3. Salvation is a free gift from God. "My *salvation and my honour depend on God; he is my mighty rock, my refuge.* [Psalm 62:7]. Though a free gift, salvation is received as a result of one positioning oneself before God by being righteous [through believing in Jesus].
4. Salvation is available for everyone on earth. " *May God be gracious to us and bless us and make his face shine upon us, that your ways may be known on earth, your salvation among all nations. [Psalm 67:1-2]*
5. Salvation is not for rejoicing on earth alone but continues even after death. The Bible describes this as follows;—"*The Sovereign Lord will wipe away the tears from all faces; He will remove the disgrace of his people from all the earth. The Lord has spoken. In that day they will say, "Surely this is our God; we trusted in him, and he saved us. This is the Lord, we trusted in him; let us rejoice and be glad in his salvation." [Isaiah 25:8-9]*
6. It is the responsibility of those who have already received their salvation to make it known to those who might not be aware otherwise. The Bible says, "*How beautiful on the mountains are the feet of those who bring good news, who proclaim peace, who*

bring good tidings, who proclaim salvation, who say to Zion, "Your God reigns!" [Isaiah 52:7].

JESUS THE LIGHT

Jesus is sometimes referred to in the Bible as "The Light", revealing God. In literal definition, a light is an electromagnetic radiation by which things are visible. In other words, light makes other substances visible to the human eye.

Many people who encounter near-death experiences talk about coming out of a dark tunnel and seeing a great light.

There are a number of occurrence where God by His divine arrangements Has also reveal to some individuals in a vision, glimpses of what is on the other side of the world (life in eternity). Almost everybody who has had such encounter also talks about the "great Light".

The questions here are "What is this great light?" and "Where do people go after death?"

The answer, explaining this great mystery, is found in the Bible.

The Word became Flesh

"In the beginning, (before all time) was the Word, [Jesus Christ] *And the Word was with God, and the Word was God Himself.*

He was present originally with God.

All things were made and came into existence through Him:

And without Him was not even one thing made that has come into existence".

In Him was Life and the Life was the Light of men.
And the light shines on in the darkness, for the darkness has Never overpowered it [put it out, or absorbed it, or appropriated
It]. There *it was—the true Light then came into the World (The genuine, perfect steadfast Light) that illumines every person. He came into the world, and though the world was made through Him, the world did not recognise Him [John 1:1-5]*

The above passage explains clearly why people, when they are close to death (or shedding the outer cover which makes them visible on earth), often see a dark tunnel and a bright light at the end of that tunnel.

Journey through life—proceeding from the known to the unknown

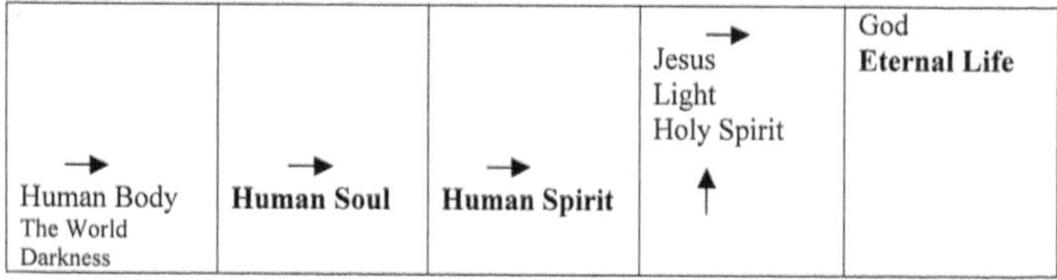

As shown in the diagram, when a person is close to death, the human soul and the human spirit move out of the human body. This transition takes the soul and the spirit through a tunnel of darkness. The Holy Spirit then assists this person, if a Christian, to enter into the Light. This happens through Jesus, who is the way to eternal life (where God is).

Thomas, one of the disciples of Jesus said to him, "Lord, we don't know where you are going, so how can we know the way?"

Jesus answered, "I am the way and the truth and the life. No one comes to the Father except through me. [John 14:5-6]

The Bible explains this by saying; "*The Word of God* (known also as Jesus) *is a lamp unto my feet*" [Psalm 119:105]. This means that it is Jesus who guides our footsteps to God.

The Word of God as written in the book of John says: *This is the verdict: Light has come into the world, but men loved darkness instead of Light because their deeds were evil.* [John 3:19] *When Jesus spoke again to the people, he said, "I am the light of the world. Whoever follows me will never walk in darkness, but will have the light of life." I have come into the world as a light, so that no one who believes in me should stay in darkness.* [John 8: 12]

The above illustrations and passages explain that the virtuous woman is on a journey through life, surrounded by darkness. In order to make it to her destination (to God) after death, the woman has to find light. Individuals have to work on the unity of their soul and spirit in order to receive Jesus.

As we read earlier, when God created human beings, He gave them free will. Although God does not wish for anyone on earth to perish, His hands are tied when it comes to the subject of free will. The reason is that He gave human beings free will to choose 'darkness' or 'Light'; to choose between the evil pleasures in this world or the perfect 'Light' (Jesus) that shows the way to life eternal.

TIPS

1. Darkness usually is associated with wickedness, which causes fear. Overcome your fears by opening your 'spiritual door' to Jesus who is already waiting at the entrance of your heart with light. This is achieved by praying the "sinners prayer".
   "Behold, I stand at the door and knock. If anyone hears My voice and opens the door, I will come in to her (him) and dine with her and she with Me. To the person who overcomes I will grant to sit with Me on My throne, as I also overcame and sat down with My Father on His throne. "He who has an ear let her (him) hear what the Spirit says to the churches." [Revelation 3:20-22]
2. Another way of receiving "light" into your spiritual being is by reading the Bible or the word of God. "*Your word is a lamp to my feet and a light for my path*". [Psalm 119:105]
3. If one is in the dark, light reveals hidden treasures, so make it a point to find out how much you are worth in the light of God. Find your "Treasures in Heaven". The Bible describes this as follows:
   "Do not store up for yourselves treasures on earth, where moth and rust destroy, and where thieves break in and steal. But store up for yourselves treasures in heaven, where moth and rust do not destroy, and where thieves do not break in and steal. For where your treasure is, there your heart will be also. "The eye is the lamp of the body. If your eyes are good, your whole body will be full of light. But if your eyes are bad, your whole body will be full of darkness. If

then the light within you is darkness, how great is that darkness!" [*Matthew 6:19-23*]

4. Most thieves operate in the dark, except the well-organised ones. Don't be a pray to the devil and his agents. They are more likely to steal your talents and gifts if you are not walking in the "Light of God". The Bible says "*The thief comes only to steal and kill and destroy; I* [Jesus] *have come that they may have life, and have it to the full*". [*John 10:10*]
5. Any time a male friend wants to invite you to a dark place, don't hesitate to ask him of his motives. Remember evil is always associated with darkness.
6. When driving in the night, light becomes a vital tool for direction, so never drive the vehicle of your life in the dark. No one knows what tomorrow holds. You will be doing yourself a great favour by getting spiritual insight.

PRAYER

After salvation, the next stage is to have daily fellowship with the Holy Spirit, the Son and the Father.

As Paul wrote in his epistle to The Romans, "*Therefore, I urge you, brethren, in view of God's mercy, to offer your bodies as living sacrifices, holy and pleasing to God—this is your spiritual act of worship.* [*Romans 12:1*]

This simply means for us to be able to relate with God and worship Him daily, as He deserves, in the Holy of Holies. We have to gain access from the body into the spiritual realm.

Prayer, which is a necessity in worship, and making our request known before God, is depicted as follows, moving and gaining access from the body on earth into the throne room of God [the Holy of Holies].

BODY	SOUL	HUMAN SPIRIT + HOLY SPIRIT	JESUS	GOD
Using the Blood of Jesus	Using the Name of Jesus	Ask the Holy Spirit to assist your Human Spirit in prayer	Having perfect standing before God like Jesus	Worshiping God in the Holy of Holies like Jesus

ACCESS FROM THE BODY INTO THE SOULISH REALM

This exercise demands the pleading of the blood of Jesus. The blood that Jesus [the son of God] shed at the Calvary cross cleanses us from our infirmities. It cleanses us from the filthiness and the corruption of this world, because without holiness no man can ascend to the holy hill of the Creator.

"Who may ascend the hill of the LORD? Who may stand in His holy place? He who has clean hands and a pure heart, who does not lift up his soul to an idol or swear by what is false". [Psalm 24:3-4]

The blood of animals in the olden days was used as atonement for sin, but the blood of Jesus, shed when he was crucified, has fully eradicated the shedding of animal's blood used for purification. This is explained in the following Bible passages: -

"Any man of the house of Israel, or of the strangers who dwell among you, who eats blood, I will set My face against that person, and will cut him off from among his people. For the life of the flesh is in the blood, and I have given it to you upon the altar to make atonement for your souls; for it is the blood that makes atonement for the soul.' Therefore I said to the children of Israel, 'No one among you shall eat blood, nor shall any stranger who dwells among you eat blood." "Any man of the children of Israel, or of the strangers who dwell among you, who hunts and catches any animal or bird that may be eaten, he shall pour out its blood and cover it with dust; for it is the life of all flesh. Its blood sustains its life. Therefore I said to the children of Israel, 'you shall not eat the blood of any flesh, for the life of all flesh is its blood. Whoever eats it shall be cut off.' [Leviticus 17:10-14]

This law was ceremonial, and is now no longer in force; the coming of the substance does away with the shadow. The blood of beasts is no longer the ransom, but Christ's blood only; therefore there is now no reason for abstaining from blood from animal flesh. The blood is now allowed for the nourishment of our bodies; it is no longer appointed to make atonement for the soul. The blood of Christ alone makes atonement.

TIPS

1. The blood of Jesus when pleaded in prayer over any sinful act such as immorality, impurity, indecency, idolatry, sorcery, enmity, strife, jealousy, anger, selfishness, division, party spirit [sects with peculiar opinions or heresies], as described in the book of Galatians 5:19, brings purification.

2. The blood of Jesus helps us to gain access into a holy place in prayer. This is described in the following passage:—"*And where these have been forgiven, there is no longer any sacrifice for sin. Therefore, brothers, since we have confidence to enter the Most Holy Place by the blood of Jesus, by a new and living way opened for us through the curtain, that is, his body". [Hebrews 10:18-20]*
3. Confessing our sins and asking for the blood of Jesus to purify us helps us to relate positively to others. "*If we claim to have fellowship with him yet walk in the darkness, we lie and do not live by the truth. But if we walk in the light, as he is in the light, we have fellowship with one another, and the blood of Jesus, his Son, purifies us from all sin. If we claim to be without sin, we deceive ourselves and the truth is not in us. [1 John 1:6-8]*
4. The pleading of the blood of Jesus in prayer helps us to overcome our own sinful desires. "*Let no one say when he is tempted, "I am tempted by God"; for God cannot be tempted by evil, nor does He Himself tempt anyone. But each one is tempted when he is drawn away by his own desires and enticed". [James 1:13-14]*
5. The blood of Jesus symbolised the covenant of God with mankind. ""*This is my blood of the covenant, which is poured out for many," he said to them. [Mark 14:24]*
6. Pleading the blood of Jesus brings justification.

Much more then, being now justified by his blood, we shall be saved from wrath through him. For if, when we were enemies, we were reconciled to God by the death of his Son, much more, being reconciled, we shall be saved by his life". [Romans 5:9-10]

ACCESS FROM THE SOULISH REALM INTO THE SPIRITUAL REALM

Using the blood of Jesus is for individual cleansing to persevere from the fleshly realm [body] into the realm of the soul. Mentioning the name "Jesus" to bring His presence in prayer enables one to gain access from the realm of the soul into the spiritual. Just like calling the name of another person, mentioning, "Jesus" brings him on the scene, and although we don't see Him appearing with our physical eyes, we believe He responds any time His name is mentioned in prayer. As such, if there are any demonic forces hindering your progress, because of the power and authority associated with that name, demons, principalities, powers and rulers on earth have no other choice but to bow when He appears. The book of Ephesians describes this wrestling as follows:—"*For we do not wrestle against flesh and blood, but against principalities, against powers, against the rulers of the darkness of this age, against spiritual hosts of wickedness in the heavenly places. [Ephesians 6:12]*

Using the authority in the "Name" that is above every name completes this exercise. The word of God says. "*At the name of Jesus every knee should bow, in heaven and on earth and under the earth, and every tongue confess that Jesus Christ is Lord, to the glory of God the Father".*
[Philippians 2:10-11]

TIPS

1. The spiritual realm is as real as the physical. Just as using keys allows us to gain access in the natural world, using the name of "Jesus" will give you entrance into the spiritual realm and then into the Holy of Holies.
2. Gaining access into the spiritual realm will provoke evil confrontations, so make sure you have been given authorisation by Jesus to enter [make sure you have confessed your sins and pleaded the blood of Jesus for purification]. The Bible explains this as follows:—

   "*Some Jews who went around driving out evil spirits tried to invoke the name of the Lord Jesus over those who were demon-possessed. They would say, "In the name of Jesus, whom Paul preaches, I command you to come out." Seven sons of Sceva, a Jewish chief priest, were doing this. (One day) the evil spirit answered them, "Jesus I know, and I know about Paul, but who are you?" Then the man who had the evil spirit jumped on them and overpowered them all. He gave them such a beating that they ran out of the house naked and bleeding". [Acts 19:13-16]*

   If sensitive in the spiritual realm, sometimes when praying for others one can perceive exactly which evil spirit is in operation. If this happens, be bold enough to rebuke that spirit in the name of Jesus. Some commonly known spirits that oppress people are the spirits of infirmity, infidelity, poverty, anger, suicide etc.
3. The name of Jesus delivers people form evil spirits. Praying for others in person sometimes makes that

person manifest in strange ways depending on the kind of evil spirit which is in operation. If this happens be not afraid. Continue to use the name of Jesus to rebuke that spirit until the person is totally delivered. The Bible gives an example in the following passage "*She kept this up for many days. Finally Paul became so troubled that he turned around and said to the spirit, "In the name of Jesus Christ I command you to come out of her!" "At that moment the spirit left her". [Acts 16:18]*

4. Ensure you highly esteem the name of Jesus before engaging in spiritual battles. An example is found in the following passage "*When this became known to the Jews and Greeks living in Ephesus, they were all seized with fear, and the name of the Lord Jesus was held in high honour. Many of those who believed now came and openly confessed their evil deeds. A number who had practised sorcery brought their scrolls together and burned them publicly.* [Acts 19: 17-19]
5. The name of Jesus, if used in an unadulterated way, brings healing to our bodies when sick. "*Then Peter said, "Silver or gold I do not have, but what I have I give you. In the name of Jesus Christ of Nazareth, walk."[Acts 3:6]*
6. The name of Jesus gives us so many victories in the spiritual realm as well as in the physical.

ACCESS INTO THE SPIRITUAL REALM BY THE HELP OF THE HOLY SPIRIT

The Bible states, when we pray with the help of the Holy Spirit we build ourselves up in faith.

"But you, dear friends, build yourselves up in your most holy faith and pray in the Holy Spirit. Keep yourselves in God's love as you wait for the mercy of our Lord Jesus Christ to bring you to eternal life". [Jude 1:20-21]

Praying for yourself or somebody else has to be done by faith because it is a request made unto God. Anything that is not done in faith is displeasing to Him and as such does not yield any profit.

"And without faith it is impossible to please God, because anyone who comes to him must believe that he exists and that he rewards those who earnestly seek him. [Hebrews 11:6]

Prayer should be done as the Holy Spirit gives us utterance. This is explained as follows:—

"Praying always with all prayer and supplication in the Spirit, being watchful to this end with all perseverance and supplication for all the saints" [Ephesians 6:18]

Speaking in other tongues, or in another language which one cannot comprehend with natural abilities, is inevitable when, one is filled with the Holy Spirit.

"All of them were filled with the Holy Spirit and began to speak in other tongues as the Spirit enabled them". [Acts 2:4]

TIPS

1. The Holy Spirit assists us to gain access into the presence of God. Sometimes when praying in the Holy Spirit for a while, there comes a point when you are no longer conscious of things around you. At times like this, if sensitive, one receives answers to problems and new revelations. "*Do not*

cast me from your presence or take your Holy Spirit from me. [Psalm 51:11]

2. If care is not taken, our rebellion can grieve the Holy Spirit. For example, if one is angry with another person, or if one has sinned in one way or the other, when in prayer, there will be no connection at all with the Holt Spirit, until such sin has been confessed and dealt with, by asking for forgiveness.
   "*Yet they rebelled and grieved His Holy Spirit. So He turned and became their enemy and He himself fought against them.[Isaiah 63:10]*
3. Whenever you are in trouble or brought to trial due to your belief in God, do not worry beforehand about what to say. The Bible advises us to just say whatever is given to us at the time, because it will not be us speaking, but the Holy Spirit. If we daily exercise our faith in the Spirit of God, He guides us and impresses on our heart what and when to speak if faced with opposition "*For the Holy Spirit will teach you at that time what you should say.*" *[Luke 12:12]*
4. When the Holy Spirit comes over us, the power of God overshadows us. This gives insight into things and sometimes the ability to perceive evil thoughts in others. If you do perceive the evil thoughts of others, in most cases it is just for you to pray about it and not to confront the person. God is all knowing so He always reveals if He overshadows somebody with His presence.

"The angel answered, "The Holy Spirit will come upon you, and the power of the Most High will overshadow you. [Luke 1:35]

5. The Holy Spirit in most cases reveals future events. This can happen in a dream or in a vision. Sometimes it comes in a form of intuition [an inner knowing]. If this revelation is something evil, pray about it because He reveals it to redeem or prepare us of adversities ahead.
   "*I only know that in every city the Holy Spirit warns me that prison and hardships are facing me*".
   [Acts 20:23]
6. Any time you are reading the Bible or doing something you don't really understand, a simple prayer such as, "Holy Spirit please give me the real meaning or revelation", will brings Him on the scene if one has already received salvation [if one has prayed the sinner's prayer]. The Bible says, The Holy Spirit is our Counsellor. Jesus said, "*But the Counsellor, the Holy Spirit, whom the Father will send in my name, will teach you all things and will remind you of everything I have said to you*".
   [John 14:26]

ACCESS INTO THE HOLY OF HOLIES WITH JESUS [THE WORD OF GOD]

Jesus, or the "The Word of God" as He is known, brings us to the throne room of mercy [the Holy of Holies] where God sees everybody who enters as His dear sons and daughters [justified by Jesus]. This is explained as follows:

"*On that day you will realise that I am in my Father, and you are in me, and I am in you. Whoever has my commands and obeys them, he is the one who loves me. He who loves me will be loved by my Father, and I too will love him and show myself to him.*" *[John 14:20-21]*

When someone enters the Holy of Holies, Jesus overshadows that person standing before God. Any request that is being made passes directly through Jesus to the Father and that is why prayer and supplications should always be made in the name of Jesus to the Father. A simple statement such as, "I pray in Jesus name", at the end of your supplication delivers your request directly before God. The Bible describes this as follows:—

Jesus said, "*Though I have been speaking figuratively, a time is coming when I will no longer use this kind of language but will tell you plainly about my Father. In that day you will ask in my name. I am not saying that I will ask the Father on your behalf. No, the Father himself loves you because you have loved me and have believed that I came from* God". [John 16:25-27]

THE LORD'S PRAYER

"*This, then, is how you should pray: Our Father in heaven, hallowed be your name, your kingdom come, your will be done on earth as it is in heaven. Give us today our daily bread. Forgive us our debts, as we also have forgiven our debtors. And lead us not into temptation, but deliver us from the evil one. For if you forgive men when they sin against you, your heavenly Father will also forgive you. But if you do not forgive men their sins, your Father will not forgive your sins.*
[Matthew 6:9-15]

The Lord's Prayer, which is usually prayed cooperatively, can also serve as a guide to how individual prayers could be conducted. Just as one moves from the known [body on earth into the throne room of God], one can proceed by dealing with the sinful nature on earth [verse 14 and 15] before moving upwards to reverencing and hallowing the name of the Father [verse 9].

Once again, using the illustration below will help us to understand the Lord's Prayer better, and demonstrate how to conduct our own individual prayers by moving from category A—E.

THE LORD'S PRAYER [Matthew 6:9-15]

E	GOD	Reverencing and worshipping the Father [verse 9]
D	JESUS	Making supplications according to the will of God through Jesus [verse 10]
C	HUMAN SPIRIT + HOLY SPIRIT	The Holy spirit assisting the human spirit to understand which needs (our own, and those of others) are in the will of God [verse 11 and 12]
B	SOUL	Using the name of Jesus to dispose of demonic powers that torment the soul. [verse 13]
A	BODY	Confession of sins and pleading the blood of Jesus for purification for sinful acts towards our brethren. [verse14 and 15]

DEALING WITH SIN (A)

Sinful conduct of the body on earth needs to be tackled any time one enters into prayer:—"*For if you*

forgive men when they sin against you, your heavenly Father will also forgive you. But if you do not forgive men their sins, your Father will not forgive your sins.
[Matthew 6:14-15]

To proceed in prayer, confessing of sins and pleading for the blood of Jesus is essential. Sometimes consciously or unconsciously we do offend our brethren. Dealing with unresolved issues with others and pleading the blood of Jesus on sinful acts will give access through this human barrier.

As mentioned earlier, access is gained from the body into the realm of the soul by confessing our sins and pleading the blood of Jesus on our bad conduct.

DEALING WITH EVIL (B)

The next category in prayer is using the name of Jesus to overcome and dispose of the devil and those demonic powers that hinder human beings and entice us with evil. "*And lead us not into temptation, but deliver us from the evil one [Matthew 6:13]*. Using the name of Jesus, as mentioned earlier, will give access from the realm of the soul, where the devil attacks and hinders prayer, into the spiritual realm. All authority on heaven and earth has been given to Jesus after his death and resurrection so using his name in prayer enables us to break through all forces, including our own evil desires that are difficult to subdue.

ASKING FOR THE ASSISTANCE OF THE HOLY SPIRIT (C)

Asking the Holy Spirit to assist the human spirit in prayer will help sieve petitions and supplications for personal needs and needs of others. "*Give us today our daily bread. "Forgive us our debts, as we also have forgiven our debtors. [Matthew 6:11- 12].* In most cases, because we live in a materialistic world, it is extremely difficult to differentiate between the things we need, and the things we want. The Holy Spirit, who searches the mind of Christ, always knows what is best for us; it is therefore vital to always engage Him when praying for our needs.

SUPPLICATION THROUGH JESUS (D)

This part of prayer occurs when one presents prayer request through Jesus to the Father. At this stage it all about asking for the will of the Father to be done in our lives and others. Here, the prayer is for the Father to let His will be done on earth [let His will for your life and others be done on earth] *"Your kingdom come, your will be done on earth as it is in heaven. [Matthew 6:10]*

REVERENCE (E)

The last stage allows us to enter the Holy of Holies under the shadow of our Lord and saviour Jesus; into the presence of the Father.

This stage in prayer is all about reverence, worship and adoration. Here the person praying addresses God as "our Father" [The Father of Jesus and the person praying]. At this stage it is all about reverencing His Holy name. This stage is really enjoyable because it incorporates the whole being of that person [spirit, soul and body]. If reverencing through a song, the words are sung with meaning and admiration. If it is just words of adoration, the spirit of God sometimes drops different words into the person's spirit to make worshiping the Father more real. This part of prayer is all about who our heavenly father is. Searching through old hymns gives evidence as to how people of old have used songs to reverence the heavenly Father. Most passages in the Bible also are a good source, to find words of adoration to worship the Father. "*Our Father in heaven, hallowed be your name, [Matthew 6:9].*

Prayer can take any form, but the most important aspect of it all is to deal with the sinful nature. Without that, the connection will not be there to proceed.

ANSWERS TO PRAYERS

From experience, answers to prayer come in three different categories.

The first is getting an answer immediately to a prayer.

The second one is the "watch and pray" kind of answer. With this kind of prayer, answers are not delivered immediately due to the infinite wisdom of the Almighty. This could drag on for weeks, months or sometimes even years. The key point here is not to give up or faint because there could be a number of reasons why it is vital for the person to wait. If a prayer is in line with the word of God [the Bible], then never feel tired making your supplications before the Father, for the Bible says, "*Ask and it will be given to you; seek and you will find; knock and the door will be opened to you. For everyone who asks receives; he who seeks finds; and to him who knocks, the door will be opened.* [Matthew 7:7-8]

The third answer is the "No" answer. God by His infinite wisdom created each one of us for a purpose. There are some things, which look good on the surface, but deep down could cause deep harm if the person was to possess them. An obvious example is to pray for a huge amount of money. To begin with, even from our limited understanding, it is not everyone on earth who will own great wealth. Secondly, inherited money, if not handled properly, could place the person in a worse situation than she was before. With all prayer requests, seek guidance from the Bible to find out what is in the will of God for your life. If you believe God has given you a vision worth a million pounds, then by all means continue to pray for the millions until your prayers are answered.

One aspect of prayer, which we should continue unceasingly, is "God, let your will be done on earth as it is in heaven". For the prayer of the righteous is powerful and effective. The Bible explains this in the following passages: -

"Therefore confess your sins to each other and pray for each other so that you may be healed. The prayer of a righteous man is powerful and effective". [James 5:16]

The Bible also tells us that God is looking for people to stand in the gap to pray for the healing of the nations.

"If my people, which are called by my name, shall humble themselves, and pray, and seek my face, and turn from their wicked ways; then will I hear from heaven, and will forgive their sin, and will heal their land". [2 Chronicles 7:14]

THINGS TO REMEMBER

- Mankind was created in the likeness of the Trinity—the human spirit, soul and body were created to relate and reflect God in three Persons [God the Father, Jesus the Son and the Holy Spirit].
- God created the human spirit in His image, for fellowship and daily communion.
- In order for the human soul not to perish in eternity, Jesus came to guide mankind to make the right choices in life, out of its own free will. This is known as 'Salvation'.
- The human body was created as a vessel for the Holy Spirit to dwell, and to carry out the work of God on earth.
- Past emotions, such as anger, fear, bitterness and lack of forgiveness, will darken the human mind and stop a woman from fulfilling the plan and purpose ordained by God, unless her mind is renewed by the word of God.
- Prayer is an effective tool, which one can use to relate to God the Father, and it can be done anywhere and at any time.
- Make a point of finding a quiet place for reading the Bible and prayer at home. Also, if spiritual growth is required, choose a regular time each day to study and pray.
- God is looking for people who will continuously pray for the healing of the nations. If you perceive in your spirit that you are called to take up this

challenge, then answer your call by devoting a time each day to praying for people and nations.

THE FATHER IS LOOKING FOR PEOPLE TO FULFIL THE FOLLOWING VISION

Joy of the Redeemed

The desert and the parched land will be glad; the wilderness will rejoice and blossom. Like the crocus, it will burst into bloom; it will rejoice greatly and shout for joy. The glory of Lebanon will be given to it, the splendour of Carmel and Sharon; they will see the glory of the LORD, the splendour of our God. Strengthen the feeble hands; steady the knees that give way; Say to those with fearful hearts, "Be strong, do not fear; your God will come, he will come with vengeance; with divine retribution he will come to save you."

Then will the eyes of the blind be opened and the ears of the deaf unstopped. Then will the lame leap like a deer, and the mute tongue shout for joy. Water will gush forth in the wilderness and streams in the desert. The burning sand will become a pool, the thirsty ground, bubbling springs. In the haunts where jackals once lay, grass and reeds and papyrus will grow. And a highway will be there; it will be called the Way of Holiness. The unclean will not journey on it; it will be for those who walk in that Way; wicked fools will not go about on it. No lion will be there, nor will any ferocious beast get up on it; they will not be found there. But only the redeemed will walk there, and the ransomed of the LORD will return. They will enter Zion with singing; everlasting joy will crown their heads. Gladness and joy will overtake them, and sorrow and sighing will flee away. [Isaiah 35:1-10]

Chapter Seven

KNOWING GOD
DEFINITIONS OF GOD
TITHES AND OFFERING
HELL (THE WORLD OF THE DEAD)
HELL (THE LAKE OF FIRE)
THINGS TO REMEMBER

KNOWING GOD

Knowing God can be compared to relating to our earthly father or mother. The longer we live with our parents, the more we learn who they are and how they deal with different issues in life. Jesus Christ, the Son of God, came down on earth to show mankind how to live a better life and in doing so, relate to God.

"Therefore if any person, is in Christ, he is a new creation; the old spiritual condition has passed away. Behold, the fresh and new has come!" *[2 Corinthians 5:17]*

The above passage helps us to understand that the responsibility for the renewal of the mind is entirely individual's responsibility. It is just like studying for examinations; in order to succeed, the correct knowledge is required. All previous misconceptions should be replaced with accurate information before the candidate stands any chance at all. In order for the virtuous woman to be a successful follower of Christ, she must first understand God's word before she can apply the "knowledge" to her life.

This transformation cannot be achieved overnight, just as lifetime experience is not gathered in a single day. One has to constantly acknowledge God and accept "His way" of leading a wholesome lifestyle in this troubled and challenging world in which we live.

By regularly reading the Bible, one will come to understand God's will and message. Constantly, putting the message into practice in everyday life, will help the virtuous woman to achieve a happier and more fulfilling lifestyle.

Therefore, get rid of all moral filth and the evil that is so prevalent and humbly accept the word planted in you, which can save you. Do not merely listen to the Word, and so deceive yourselves. Do what it says. Anyone who listens to the Word but does not do what it says is like a person, who looks at her face in a mirror and, after looking at herself, goes away and immediately forgets what she looks like. [*James 1:21-24*]

Virtuous woman, it is only after renewing your mind, can you understand who God really is. The Bible tells us that human beings have no excuse for making the journey through life without knowing God.

"*Since what may be known about God is plain to them, because God has made it plain to them. For since the creation of the world God's invisible qualities, his eternal power and divine nature have been clearly seen, being understood from what has been made, so that men are without excuse.*

Foralthoughthey knewGod, theyneitherglorifiedhimas Godnorgave thankstohim, buttheirthinkingbecamefutile and their foolish hearts were darkened". *[Romans 1:19-21]*

Whilst human beings are on this planet, they have a responsibility (and an obligation) to discover certain truths. Such as, "who created them?" Why they are here and where heading. If they fail to discover the answers, before the end of their days, they only have themselves to blame. The whole point of creation was to serve as a constant reminder to us of the power and wonder, of God.

How to renew your mind and follow Jesus' teachings

1. By knowing who God is.
2. By acknowledging God through Jesus.
3. By Praising God.
4. By allowing the Holy Spirit to direct your path daily

Definitions of God

- God is everywhere (omnipresent)
- God is all—powerful (omnipotent)
- God knows everything (omniscient)

Below are some examples of who God is according to the Bible, along with explanations of what God means, to the virtuous woman.

WHO GOD IS (according to the Bible)	**WHO GOD IS (to the virtuous woman)**
God is Love	My God
God is Righteous	My Redeemer
God is Compassionate	My fortress
God is Faithful	My Rock
God is Good	My Shepherd
God is Powerful	My Shield
God is Merciful	My Creator
God is Kind	My Strength
God is Holy	My Maker
God is All Knowing	My Confidence
God is Eternal	My Salvation
God is Everlasting	The Lover of my soul
God the Almighty	The Joy of my Exaltation

Knowing God gives hope, strength and a sense of security. This knowledge gives insight to the virtuous woman of "His ways" and how to accept His plan for her life.

Knowing God will enable you to relate to Him better in all areas of your life. The reference to this is easily found, in the dialogue God had with Moses.

"Moses said to God, "suppose I go to the Israelites (Your people) and say to them, The God of your fathers has sent me to you, and they ask me, what is his name? Then what shall I tell them?"

God said to Moses, "I AM WHO I AM". This is what you are to say to the Israelites: "I AM" has sent me to you. God also said to Moses, say to the Israelites, The LORD, The God of your fathers—the God of Abraham, the God of Isaac and the God of Jacob—has sent me to you. This is my name forever, the name by which I am to be remembered from generation to generation. [Exodus 3: 13-15]

TIPS

1. God is the creator of Heaven and Earth.
2. God created Human Beings and Animals from the beginning.
3. God created the air.
4. God made the sun, moon and the stars.
5. God made the oceans, mountains and the valleys.
6. God created all trees and vegetations.

God in revealing Himself as "I AM", means that *He* can operate in many different ways depending on how an individual relates to Him.

For example, for financial breakthrough, if the woman relates to God by obeying His commandment in giving, to reach out to the lost souls, for such an individual God will reveal Himself as, " The Provider"—["I AM GOD YOUR PROVIDER"].

Tithes and offering.

The Bible makes it clear to us that as followers of Christ it's our responsibilities to ensure the work Jesus started on earth is carried out to the uttermost parts of the earth. Christians, using their talents and resources to minister to different people who are yet to know about Christ, will achieve these aims and objectives.

The great commission is explained in the following passage:—

"*Then Jesus came to them and said, "All authority in heaven and on earth has been given to me. Therefore go and make disciples of all nations, baptizing them in the name of the Father and of the Son and of the Holy Spirit, and teaching*

them to obey everything I have commanded you. And surely I am with you always, to the very end of the age."
[Matthew 28:18-20]

The Great commission invites everyone who is a believer of Christ to reach out to others with the Gospel.

Everyone on earth has a part to play in the bigger picture but unfortunately only few discover the plan, purpose and the significance of their existence. "The Great commission", once again is based on individual's choices. God by his infinite wisdom has given each individual the freedom to make their own choices and reap the consequences.

This freedom of choice have ruined many lives but God being so merciful, always device another route to assist mankind to evaluate their own actions.

"I the Lord do not change. So you, O descendants of Jacob, are not destroyed. Ever since the time of your forefathers you have turned away from my decrees and have not kept them. Return to me, and I will return to you," says the Lord Almighty. "But you ask, 'How are we to return?' Will a man rob God? Yet you rob me. But you ask, 'How do we rob you?' "In tithes and offerings. You are under a curse the whole nation of you because you are robbing me. Bring the whole tithe into the storehouse that there may be food in my house. Test me in this," says the Lord Almighty, "and see if I will not throw open the floodgates of heaven and pour out so much blessing that you will not have room enough for it. I will prevent pests from devouring your crops, and the vines in your fields will not cast their fruit," says the Lord Almighty. [Malachi 3:6-11]

Given towards the work of God can be done in so many different ways. The fundamental rule is to spread the Gospel of Jesus Christ and to care for the needy. Individual resources can be given to any church organisation, observing this basic rule or as an individual; you can set a tithe [10%] of your earnings aside to care for the disadvantaged in your community or anywhere in the world. The Word of God explain this further, as follows:

"When the Son of Man comes in his glory, and all the angels with him, he will sit on his throne in heavenly glory. All the nations will be gathered before him, and he will separate the people one from another as a shepherd separates the sheep from the goats. He will put the sheep on his right and the goats on his left.

The King will reply, I tell you the truth: whatever you did for one of the least of these brothers of mine, you did for me.

Then he will say to those on his left, 'Depart from me, you who are cursed, into the eternal fire prepared for the devil and his angels. For I was hungry and you gave me nothing to eat, I was thirsty and you gave me nothing to drink, I was a stranger and you did not invite me in, I needed clothes and you did not clothe me, I was sick and in prison and you did not look after me. They also will answer, 'Lord, when did we see you hungry or thirsty or a stranger or needing clothes or sick or in prison, and did not help you?' He will reply, 'I tell you the truth, whatever you did not do for one of the least of these, you did not do for me. Then they will go away to eternal punishment, but the righteous to eternal life." [*Matthew 25:31-46*]

Whatever you need, God is saying to this generation as He said to Moses "I AM…."

All you have to do is fill in those blanks by searching the scriptures and doing what the Bible teaches, regarding that particular issue.

There are so many people in need of essential commodities of life and the truth is, there are more than enough resources to go round the whole world, if everybody is to act as a good steward of what God has entrusted to mankind.

As David wrote in the book of Psalms, knowing God intimately helps us not to lean on our own understanding but rather to look beyond our human limitations and see the Supreme Being who is capable of doing all things. Psalm 23, gives us hope and encouragement for the future. It gives understanding of who God is and what He can do for us if only we could put our trust in Him.

Psalm 23, A Psalm of David Psalms
[God supplies my needs]

The LORD is my shepherd I shall not be in want. He makes me lie down in green pastures, he leads me beside quiet waters, he restores my soul. He guides me in paths of righteousness for his name's sake. Even though I walk through the valley of the shadow of death, I will fear no evil, for you are with me; your rod and your staff, they comfort me. You prepare a table before me in the presence of my enemies. You anoint my head with oil; my cup overflows. Surely goodness and love will follow me all the days of my life, and I will dwell in the house of the LORD forever". [Psalm 23:1-6]

TIPS

1. Any form of "given", whether your time, energy, money or talent can be compared to a seed, which if planted in a good soil will eventually geminate and produce a harvest. This principle is set from the foundation of the earth and cannot be altered. "*As long as the earth endures, seedtime and harvest, cold and heat, summer and winter, day and night will never cease.*" *[Genesis 8:22]*
2. Anything given to support the work of God is rewarding [has the tendency of yielding a good harvest], but God works in mysterious ways so never determine where the harvest is going to come from. The Bible explains this as follows:— "*Neither he who plants nor he who waters is anything, but only God, who makes things grows. The man who plants and the man who waters have one purpose, and each will be rewarded according to his or her own labour. For we are God's fellow workers; His field, His* building". [1 Corinthians 3:7-9]
3. Your home should be your number one priority if married. As such, providing for your children and your husband should take precedence of all your "given" towards the building of God's *kingdom. The Bible explain this as follows: -*
   "*In like manner, you married women, be submissive to your own husbands [subordinate yourselves as being secondary to and dependent on them, and adapt yourselves to them], so that even if any do not obey the Word [of God], they may be won over not by discussion but by the [godly] lives of their wives, when they observe the pure and modest way in which they conduct yourselves, together with reverence for their*

husbands. [All that reverence includes: to respect, defer to, revere him to honour, esteem, appreciate, prize, and, in the human sense, to adore him, that is, to admire, praise, be devoted to, deeply love, and enjoy your husband].
[1 Peter 3:1-2] (Amplified Bible)

4. You will be directed to a fertile soil to cultivate if you daily ask for the guidance of the Holy Spirit. A good soil is simply a project God is involved in. God is the originator of every fruitful project, destined on earth no matter how small. If you yield to His Spirit, He will always direct your path. The Bible explains this as follows:—"*The Spirit searches all things, even the deep things of God. For who among men knows the thoughts of a man except the man's spirit within him? In the same way no one knows the thoughts of God except the Spirit of God. [1 Corinthians 2:10-11]*
5. Motive for given towards the work of any ministry, should never be done, based on receiving favour from people. It should always be done merely because of your love for God. He is the one who shows favour and allows other people to do the same towards a person. In other words, the focus for the source of all things in life should be directed to God.

6. Any "given" should be done in faith. It is usually not a smooth sailing even when being led by The Spirit of God to give towards a project. Given, demands stretching your faith in most cases,

but anything done in faith is rewarding because without faith no one can please God.

When we relate to God as a Father, He responds back to us by saying "I AM GOD, your Shepherd to take good care of you".

Knowing God and acknowledging *Him* through His dear Son, Jesus, will help you to understand *His* love, mercy and goodness towards mankind.

Praising God is, therefore, born out of understanding of who He is and this will also assist you to acknowledging Him as the Creator of all things. Praise, which is part of worship, is superior to prayer. It demands walking in the will and purposes of the Creator and as such it is the totality of an individual's lifestyle. The Bible states that God takes pleasure from the praises of *His* People. This means praising God gets His attention more than prayers. Christians are therefore, responsible for living lifestyles exhibiting God's Goodness and kindness.

"But you are a chosen people, a royal priesthood, a holy nation, a people belonging to God, that you may declare the praises of him who called you out of darkness into his wonderful light. Once you were not a people, but now you are the people of God; once you had not received mercy, but now you have received mercy". [1 Peter 2:9-10]

The woman who lives in the centre of God's will, carries *His* Glory or *His* presence wherever she goes. A Worshiper [a person who carries God's Glory] is empowered to change spiritual atmosphere of wherever she goes.

A WORSHIPER

- A worshipper is someone who worships the Father in spirit and in truth. This is attained by spiritual maturity, which has been made available for all Christians. The Bible explains this as follows, "*You Samaritans worship what you do not know; we worship what we do know, for salvation is from the Jews. Yet a time is coming and has now come when the true worshipers will worship the Father in spirit and truth, for they are the kind of worshipers the Father seeks. [John 4:22-23]*
- A worshiper acknowledges God, as the Creator of heaven and earth, this adoration is usually express in songs of thanksgiving or words of admiration. " *Come, let us sing for joy to the Lord; let us shout aloud to the Rock of our salvation. Let us come before him with thanksgiving and extol him with music and song. For the Lord is the great God, the great King above all gods. In his hand are the depths of the earth, and the mountain peaks belong to him. The sea is his, for he made it, and his hands formed the dry land". [Psalm 95:1-5]*
- A Worshiper is a person, who always finds something good to praise God for, regardless of her circumstances. She knows that whilst here on earth, every situation she encounters is subject to change. She is aware that her destiny is to spend eternity with God and that supersedes any difficulties she encounters on her journey.

- A Worshiper is more concerned about her soul and spirit than her body, [her earthly suit] because she is aware that her body is the only part of her "being" she cannot take with her to eternity.

- A Worshiper takes pleasure in observing the handy-work of the Creator and expresses the wonder of creation in so many different ways. Example, can be found in the following passage "*When I consider your heavens, the work of your fingers, the moon and the stars, which you have set in place, what is man that you are mindful of him, the son of man that you care for him?*" [Psalm 8: 3-4]
- A worshiper esteems high her relationship with the Creator and as such tries her possible best not to tarnish that relationship in anyway.

Psalm 27, A Psalm of David
[God is my light and my salvation]

"The LORD is my light and my salvation whom shall I fear? The LORD is the stronghold of my life of whom shall I be afraid?

When evil men advance against me to devour my flesh, when my enemies and my foes attack me, they will stumble and fall.

Though an army besiege me, my heart will not fear; though war break out against me, even then will I be confident. One thing I ask of the Lord, this is what I seek: that I may dwell in the house of the Lord all the days of my life, to gaze upon the beauty of the Lord and to seek him in his temple. For in the day of trouble he will keep me safe in his dwelling; he will hide me in the shelter of his tabernacle and set me high upon a rock. Then my head will be exalted above the enemies who surround me;

at his tabernacle will I sacrifice with shouts of joy; I will sing and make music to the Lord.

Hear my voice when I call, O Lord; be merciful to me and answer me.

My heart says of you, "Seek his face!" Your face, Lord, I will seek.

Do not hide your face from me, do not turn your servant away in anger; you have been my helper. Do not reject me or forsake me, O God my Saviour. Though my father and mother might forsake me, the Lord will receive me. Teach me your ways, O Lord; lead me in a straight path because of my oppressors. Do not turn me over to the desire of my foes, for false witnesses rise up against me, breathing out violence. I am still confident of this: I will see the goodness of the Lord in the land of the living. Wait for the Lord; be strong and take heart and wait for the Lord [Psalm 27:1-14]

HELL (THE WORLD OF THE DEAD)

When God made human beings, He gave them their free will to choose darkness or light: to choose between the evil pleasures in this world or the perfect Light (Jesus) that shows the way to Life Eternal.

People who disobey what is written in the word of God and follow the dictates of their own soul have themselves to blame, because at the end of their journey here on earth, they will find themselves trapped in the world of the dead.

The question here is, "What happens to those who are not able to make it to the Great Light at the end of the tunnel when they die?" The answer once again is found in the Bible.

"My son, pay attention to my wisdom, listen well to my words of insight, that you may maintain discretion and your lips may preserve knowledge. For the lips of an adulteress drip honey, and her speech is smoother than oil; but in the end she is bitter as gall, sharp as a double-edged sword. Her feet go down to death; her steps lead straight to the grave. She gives no thought to the way of life; her paths are crooked, but she knows it not". [Proverbs 5:1-6]

To be more precise, let us try and locate this path, which leads to the world of the dead or Hell as most people would know it.

The above passage, as narrated from the Good News version, states that, verse 5-6 "*She will take you down to the world of the dead; the road she walks is the road to death; she does not stay on the road to Life; but wanders off, and does not even realise what is happening*".

To understand this fully, let us look at the following illustration: -

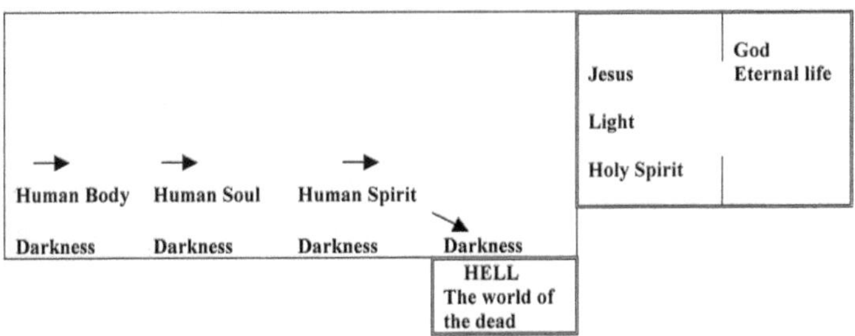

To explain the above diagram, let us look at it in conjunction with the following passage from the book of Romans.

"This righteousness from God comes through faith in Jesus Christ to all who believe. There is no difference, for all have

sinned and fall short of the glory of God, and are justified freely by his grace through the redemption that came by Christ Jesus". [Romans 3: 22-24]

Since the fall of Adam and Eve at the beginning of creation as described in the book of Genesis, any human being born into this world automatically inherits the sin nature from their parents. To be able to obtain salvation, which will lead to eternal life after death, the woman (or the person) will have to have faith in Jesus.

As illustrated, the woman who, out of her own will, decides not to accept Jesus into her life, automatically falls short of the Glory of God. This person, out of her own will has rejected God, the existence of Jesus' work on earth, his death and resurrection as well as the power of the Holy Spirit.

The above passage helps us to understand that; because of sin, we have all falling short of the Light {Jesus}, known as the Glory of God and in order, to be inline with the Holy Spirit, we have to have Faith and believe that truly Jesus is the way to the Father {God}. The woman, who does not believe in Jesus, cannot accept directions from The Holy Spirit and as such wonders off to Hell.

As described in the Bible, judgement and destination of the spirit of mankind is not for anybody to know except God. But one thing is certain the final destination of the spirit of the righteous goes up in Glory to the Creator. The death of Christ, as described in the book of Luke explain this statement.

"Jesus called out with a loud voice, "Father, into your hands I commit my spirit." When he had said this, he breathed his last". [Luke 23:46]

The book of Ezekiel, help us to also understand that God detest the death of the wicked (the sinner), and it is His greatest desire, that all should accept Christ and come into repentance before death.

"Say to them, 'As surely as I live, declares the Sovereign LORD, I take no pleasure in the death of the wicked, but rather that they turn from their ways and live. Turn! Turn from your evil ways! Why will you die, O house of Israel?" [Ezekiel 33:11]

The death of the wicked is compared to that of beast in the book of Ecclesiastes. What awaits the sinner after death is judgement and the second death.

"I said in my heart regarding the subject of the sons of men, God is trying (separating and sifting) them, that they may see that by themselves [under the sun, without God] they are but like beasts.

For that which befalls the sons of men befalls beasts; even [in the end] one thing befalls them both. As the one dies, so dies the other. Yes, they all have one breath and spirit, so that a man has no pre-eminence over a beast; for all is vanity (emptiness, falsity, and futility)! All go to one place; all are of the dust, and all turn to dust again. Who knows the spirit of man, whether it goes upward, and the spirit of the beast, whether it goes downward to the earth".

[Ecclesiastes 3:18-21] Amplified Bible

TIPS

1. Life on earth is temporal. It is something loaned to us for a season, so never get too comfortable with it. It has "strings attached", which can be pulled at anytime by the Creator. One minute a person is full of life eating, talking and laughing and in an instance, it is all over.
   "*What man can live and shall not see death, or can deliver himself from the [powerful] hand of Sheol (the place of the dead)? Selah [pause, and calmly consider that]! [Psalm 89:48]*
2. Life on earth can also be described as a breath, one second a person is breathing in and out, then all of a sudden, it is over." *Behold, You have made my days as [short as] handbreadths, and my lifetime is as nothing in Your [God's] sight. Truly every man at his best is merely a breath! Selah [pause, and think calmly of that]! [Psalm 39:5] Amplified Bible*
3. Life on earth can be compared with a passing shadow, the shadow of a person or an object is not real. The real you, is moving from a different location towards a certain destination. "*Man is like a breath; his days are like a fleeting shadow". [Psalm 144:4]*

4. Life on earth is like a flower it is beautiful to look at when it flourishes but with a short lifespan.
   "*For he knows how we are formed, he remembers that we are dust. As for man, his days are like grass, he flourishes like a flower of the field; the wind blows over it and it is gone, and its place remembers it no more. [Psalm 103:14-16]*

5. Life can also be compared to a morning mist. It appears for a while and disappears into thin air.
   "They offer human sacrifice and kiss the calf-idols. Therefore they will be like the morning mist, like the early dew that disappears, like chaff swirling from a threshing floor, like smoke escaping through a window". [Hosea 13:3]
6. Life can be compared, as a race, the most important aspect of it, is to finish and complete God's given task.
   "However, I consider my life worth nothing to me, if only I may finish the race and complete the task the Lord Jesus has given me—the task of testifying to the gospel of God's grace". [Acts 20:24]

HELL (THE LAKE OF FIRE)

Hell, or the lake of fire is Satan's final destiny. After the return of Jesus Christ and the "Judgement" day, Hell, the lake of fire will also be, the final destination for angels and human beings who sinned.

"And I saw the dead, great and small, standing before the throne, and books were opened. Another book was opened, which is the book of life. The dead were judged according to what they had done as recorded in the books. The sea gave up the dead that were in it, and Hell (The world of the dead), gave up the dead that were in them, and each person was judged according to what he had done. Then death and the world of the dead were thrown into the lake of fire. The lake of fire is the second death. If anyone's name was not found written in the book of life, she [or he] was thrown into the lake of fire".
[*Revelations 20:12-15*]

The Bible helps us to understand that, just as the world is real so is hell. The following passages from the Bible were to make the virtuous woman aware of the troubles, which may await her if she refuses to acknowledge God and do *His* will.

"I tell you, my friends, do not be afraid of those who kill the body and after that can do no more. But I will show you whom you should fear: Fear God who, after the killing of the body, has power to throw you into hell. Yes, I tell you, fear Him". *[Luke 12:4-5]*

"For if God did not spare angels when they sinned, but sent them to hell, putting them into gloomy dungeons to be held for judgment; if He did not spare the ancient world when He brought the flood on its ungodly people, but protected Noah, a preacher of righteousness, and seven others".[2 Peter 2: 4-5]

"But I tell you that anyone who looks at a woman lustfully has already committed adultery with her in his heart. If your right eye causes you to sin, gouge it out and throw it away. It is better for you to lose one part of your body than for your whole body to be thrown into hell. And if your right hand causes you to sin, cut it off and throw it away. It is better for you to lose one part of your body than for your whole body to go into hell". [Matthew 5:28-29]

Hell, or the "lake of fire" as the Bible describes it, is not a pleasant place at all. We all know how painful it is to have even a minor cut on our bodies, yet the above passage makes us understand that it is better for a person to cut off her hand and throw it away, than to wonder into the world of the dead. The pain of loosing one's hand is nothing compared to the torment of spending eternity without God's love in Hell.

Virtuous woman, would you rather await the results of your actions? Remember, there may not be time to put things right if you make mistakes, as you have embarked upon a journey (of life) to a final destination. Disbelief, will lead you to hell. The Bible says; "A *fool thinks in her heart that there is no God*", [*Psalm 14:1*], but once a person wonders off to hell there is no escape.

TIPS

1. Never listen to people who don't believe in God [The Supreme Being], yet are prepared to talk endlessly about witches and ghost. They really don't have a clue what the spiritual realm entails.
2. Death is not the final destination of human beings and as such reverence has to be given to the one who is able to destroy mankind even after death. "*Do not be afraid of those who kill the body but cannot kill the soul. Rather, be afraid of the One who can destroy both soul and body in hell. [Matthew 10:28]*
3. Never judge or condemn another person. You can correct a person in love, if you feel he or she is heading towards destruction. Judgement and condemnation however, is for God alone to decide. "*You, then, why do you judge your brother? Or why do you look down on your brother? For we will all stand before God's judgment seat*".
   [Romans 14:10]

4. After death, is judgement before Christ and this is based on lifestyle of every individual whilst on earth. "*For we must all appear before the judgment seat of Christ, that each one may receive what is due him or her for the things done while in the body, whether good or bad*". *[2 Corinthians 5:10]*
5. There is real torment in hell, which can never be compared with hardship or any kind of suffering here on earth. "*In hell, where he was in torment, he looked up and saw Abraham far away, with Lazarus by his side*. *[Luke 16:23]*
6. The following passage gives a glimpse of unquenchable fire that awaits the sinner. "*The people were waiting expectantly and were all wondering in their hearts if John might possibly be the Christ. John, answered them, "I baptise you with water. But somebody, more powerful than I will come, the thongs of whose sandals I am not worthy to untie. He will baptise you with the Holy Spirit and with fire. His winnowing fork is in his hand to clear his threshing floor and to gather the wheat into his barn, but he will burn up the chaff with unquenchable fire.*"
[Luke 3:15-17]

The Bible says; "*For God so greatly loved and dearly priced the world that He gave up His only begotten Son, so that whoever believes in Him shall not perish, but have eternal (everlasting) life*". [*John 3:16*]

To secure eternity of a glorious life with Christ, the woman has to only have faith, believe in Christ, and say the sinner's Prayers. The Bible describes this plan as follows:

"If you acknowledge and confess with your lips that Jesus is Lord and in your heart believe that God raised Him from the dead, you will be saved. For with the heart a person believes and so is justified (declared righteous, acceptable to God), and with the mouth She [or he] confesses and confirms [His] salvation".
[Romans10: 9-10].

If you have not said your sinner's prayers already, here is another opportunity for you to get it right with God.

Sinner's Prayers: -

Say the following sinners prayers aloud: -

"Dear God, I am a sinner I do not even deserve to pray to you.
But I understand that it does not matter where I am coming from.
I understand that it does not even matter what I have and have not done in the past.
I understand I can pray to you right now through your dear son Jesus Christ who, died at The Calvary Cross and you will wipe away my past and forgive me my sins.
Please forgive me in The name of Jesus and make me your child once again.
Father God, please fill me with Your Holy Spirit and make me strong not to go back to my old ways again.
In Jesus Mighty Name I pray, Amen".

THINGS TO REMEMBER

- The knowledge of God gives the woman hope, strength and a sense of security.

- Knowing, who God really is, enables the woman to obey *His* word and relate to *Him* in all areas of her needs.

- The whole of creation is a reminder to us of who God is, and mankind has no excuse not to discover this truth.

- The woman is on a journey through life to eternity but if out of her free will decides not to accept Christ she automatically, falls short of God's glory and risks eternity in Hell (the lake of fire).

Chapter Eight

THE WIDE AND THE NARROW, ROAD
THE CREATOR AND THE DECEIVER
THE FORBIDDEN FRUIT
IMMEDIATE AND AFTER—EFFECTS OF SIN

The woman, (Eve) from the formation of the earth as described in the book of Genesis, had a vital role ordained by her "Creator" to play in life. Also the man, (Adam) on the other hand was to love and care for his wife. The role of the married woman, as decreed by God, is to submit to her own husband, to assist and encourage him, until God's plan and purposes (as written in the word of God) are fulfilled in that household. Remember this does not happen overnight; it takes a lot of endurance, a lot of faith and a lot of prayers to build a home.

For the single woman, her submission is unto the Lord, until God's plan and purposes are fulfilled in her life.

Eve, the first woman mentioned in the Bible, failed this assignment miserably, by allowing herself to be deceived into thinking that personal satisfaction and material wealth were more important than spiritual growth, which bring ultimate salvation. Unfortunately, this mindset and attitude was contrary to the original plan and purposes, which God the Creator, had for mankind.

The wide and the narrow, road

We need to understand that everything created under the sun has an equal and opposite, side to it. For example, the other side to daytime is night—time and the opposite of light, is darkness. Usually, the opposite side of anything can be perceived to be in direct competition at all times. If there is light, darkness has no choice but to wait patiently until the light is switched off. Human life can be identified with this truth. Darkness is the absence of light. The word of God brings light to our lives. The absence of that light inevitably, means we are thrown into darkness, which is a symbol for the absence of God in our lives.

The foundations of life as discussed earlier, is equally important as choosing the road or pathway for your journey. How you start your journey (Things you take with you), as well as the route you decide on to get to your destination, is of utmost importance.

The Narrow and Wide Gates
Enter through the narrow gate. For wide is the gate and broad is the road that leads to destruction, and many enter through it. But small is the gate and narrow the road that leads to life, and only few find it.
Don't look for shortcuts to God. The market is flooded with sure-fire, easygoing formulas for a successful life that can be practiced in your spare time. Don't fall for those things, even though a lot of people do it. The way to life—to God

is vigorous and requires total attention. [Matthew 7: 13] Message.

As aforementioned, Jesus came to assist mankind to make the right choices in life. The woman has the gift of free will as well as many choices to make on a daily basis. Being on a journey through life, reading of "instructions" and "road maps" is crucial. If the virtuous woman wants to get to her destination as ordained by her maker, then prayer, and reading of her Bible is crucial indeed.

TIPS

1. To be on a narrow road means to be on guard for destructions, which will detour you from your original plan and purposes of life.
2. To be on a narrow road, you have to stand true to what you believe in and this means, standing alone sometimes if no one is interested in the truth.
3. To be on a narrow road, you have to be strong and courageous. You have to be able to move forward if no one is there to assist you.
4. To be on a narrow road means, not many people will be on the same pathway as you [or run with your vision].
4. To be on a narrow road demands moving forward and not looking back, if you are pioneering a project, you cannot afford to act aimlessly.
6. To be on a narrow road means everything you do must be done in love because you cannot afford to have enemies on the way.

Virtuous woman, God wants you to understand that because you are so uniquely made, for a specific purpose in *His* Plan, no one else can direct you on the way you should lead your life. Having a mentor or a spiritual authority over your life is essential, but it is an individual's choice to discover the specific reason, for your presence on earth. It is an individual's choice to discover the plan and purpose God has for her life.

The only way to fully discover the plan is to relate to the Creator himself through prayer and reading of the Bible. Not every word in the Bible is directly related to your needs but by the help of the Holy Spirit, deeper understanding will be revealed in passages, which relate directly to you as a person.

In the book of Genesis this is exactly what happened. Instead of the woman [Eve] fulfilling her destiny by submitting and encouraging the man [Adam] as God planned, rather she encouraged him to turn from his God given vision. Neither of them was attentive to instructions and neither of them took the time to relate to God to find out exactly what *He* had in mind for them.

The forbidden fruit

"The serpent was more clever than any wild animal God had made. He spoke to the Woman: Do I understand that God told you not to eat from any tree in the garden?
The Woman said to the serpent, Not at all. We can eat from the trees in the garden. It's only about the tree in the middle of the garden that God said, "Don't eat from it; don't even touch it or you'll die. The serpent told the Woman, "You won't die. God knows that the moment you eat from that tree, you'll see what's really going on. You'll be just like God,

knowing everything, ranging all the way from good to evil."
When the Woman saw that the fruit looked good to eat and realised what she would get out of it—she'd know everything!—She took and ate the fruit and then gave some to her husband, and he ate.
Immediately the two of them did "see what's really going on"-saw themselves naked! They sewed fig leaves together as makeshift clothes for themselves.
When they heard the sound of God strolling in the garden in the evening breeze, the man and his wife hid in the trees of the garden, hid from God.
God called to the Man: "Where are you?"
He said, "I heard you in the garden and I was afraid because I was naked. And I hid."
God said, "Who told you, you were naked? Did you eat from that tree I told you not to eat from?"
The Man said, "The Woman you gave me as a companion, she gave me fruit from the tree, and, yes, I ate it."
God said to the Woman, "What is this that you've done?"
The serpent seduced me, she said, "and I ate."
God told the serpent: "Because you've done this, you're cursed, cursed beyond all cattle and wild animals.
Cursed to slink on your belly
and eat dirt all your life". [Genesis 3:1-14] Amplified

TIPS

1. Sin is a torment, which has a way of making people fearful of the unknown.
2. Sin always leads to more lies and sinful acts.
3. A sinful person develops so many cunning ways, which seems wise, but when caught, one will discover it was all foolishness.

4. Sin always present itself in disguise, it is always pleasant to look at but very deadly.
5. A sinful person uses extra energy to cover up her tracks.
6. Sinful acts, attracts an audience but when caught the person stands alone for the verdict.

The woman, [Eve] decided to listen to a reptile for directions for her life, rather than from God. The man, [Adam] being as reckless and indecisive as the woman, went along with her wishes without his own judgement and acknowledgment of the word of God.

The most heartbreaking thing to say in life is "if only I had known," because at that time, it might be too late to go back. Going forward at that time could also be a problem, because you might not know when or where to turn! But thank God for Christ. So long as you are alive on earth, you can still make a better choice, by doing a U-turn, to go back and find the route you missed. At each junction along your journey you can still connect to the road marked "Jesus", because that is the only route that will take you to your destination, if you expect salvation.

Thomas said, "*Master, we have no idea where you're going. How do you expect us to know the road?" Jesus said, "I am the Road, also the Truth, also the Life. No one gets to the Father except through me. If you really knew me, you would know my Father as well. From now on, you do know Him. You've even seen Him!" [John 14:5-7]*

The Creator and The Deceiver

Virtuous woman, the immeasurable natural beauty, which surrounds you, cannot be accidental. Instead it must be the result of the labours of a Supreme Being – the handiwork of God.

The Word of God says, *Jesus came so that we can have life more in abundance, but Satan came to steal, kill and to destroy.* [*John 10:10*]

Virtuous woman, God wants you to be aware that whatever plan and purpose He has for your life, the enemy is right there presenting a false plan. Unfortunately, the choice of which master you want to follow, is entirely yours.

> *"But if your eyes are bad, your whole body will be full of darkness. If then the light within you is darkness, how great is that darkness!*
> *"No one can serve two masters. Either he will hate the one and love the other, or he will be devoted to the one and despise the other. You cannot serve both God and Money.[Matthew 6:23-24]*

The above passage clarifies that we have an enemy who does not rest, but is doing everything possible to derail and deceive children of God. The weapons which this enemy uses, to derail mankind are money, necessities of life and self-importance. This is the main reason why the Bible says, "*Money is the root of all evil"[1 Timothy 6:10], and "Pride comes before a fall"[Proverbs 16:18].*

"People who want to get rich fall into temptation and a trap and into many foolish and harmful desires that plunge men into ruin and destruction. For the love of money is a root of all kinds of evil. Some people, eager for money, have wandered

from the faith and pierced themselves with many grieves". [1 *Timothy 6:9-10*]

It is all vanity

Money and possessions are necessities for human survival on earth, but never compensate the excess of it for life eternal with Christ. As the writer of Ecclesiastes proclaimed, it is all vanity.

"Everything seems Meaningless: "Meaningless! Meaningless!" says the Teacher. "Utterly meaningless! Everything is meaningless." What do people gain from all their labour and toils under the sun? Generations come and generation goes, but the earth remains forever.

The sun rises and the Sunsets and hurries back to where it rises. The wind blows to the south and turns to the north; round and round it goes, never returning on its course. All streams flow into the sea, yet the sea is never full. To the place the streams comes from, there they return again. All things are wearisome, more than one can say. The eye never has enough of seeing, nor the ear its fill of hearing. What has been will be again, what has been done will be done again; there is nothing new under the sun. Is there anything of which one can say, "Look? This is something new"? It was here already, long ago; it was here before our time. There is no remembrance of people of old, and even those who are yet to come, will not be remembered by those who follow. (Ecclesiastes 1:2-11)

Pleasures are vanity

Pleasure doesn't have any meaning: *I said to myself, "Come on. I'll put pleasure to the test. I want to find out what is good." But that also proved to be meaningless. "Laughter is foolish," I said. "And what can pleasure do for me?" I tried cheering myself up by drinking wine. I even tried living foolishly. But wisdom was still guiding me. I wanted to see what was really important for people to do on earth during the few days of their lives. So I started some large projects. I built houses for myself. I planted vineyards. I made gardens and parks. I planted all kinds of fruit trees in them. I made lakes to water groves of healthy trees.* (Ecclesiastes 2:1-4)

Treasures are vanity

I stored up silver and gold for myself. I gathered up the treasures of kings and their kingdoms. I got some male and female singers. I also got many women for myself. Women delight the hearts of men. I became far more important than anyone in the world. And in spite of everything, I didn't lose my wisdom. I gave myself everything my eyes wanted. There wasn't any pleasure that I refused to give myself. I took delight in everything I did. And that was what I got for all of my work. But then I looked over everything my hands had done. I saw what I had worked so hard to get. And nothing had any meaning. It was like chasing the wind. Nothing was gained on this earth. (Ecclesiastes 2:8-11)

Worldly wisdom is vanity

Wisdom and foolish pleasure don't have any meaning: I decided to think about wisdom. I also thought about foolish pleasure. What more can people do? Can they do anything more than others have already done? I saw that wisdom is better than foolishness, just as light is better than darkness. The eyes of a wise person see things clearly. A person who is foolish lives in darkness. But I finally realised that death catches up with both of them. Then I thought, "What happens to a foolish person will catch up with me too. So what do I gain by being wise?" I said to myself, "That doesn't have any meaning either." Like a foolish person, a wise person won't be remembered very long. In days to come, both of them will be forgotten. Like a person who is foolish, a wise person must die too! (Ecclesiastes 2:12-16)

Excessive work is vanity

Work doesn't have any meaning: So I hated life. That's because the work that is done on this earth made me sad. None of it has any meaning. It's like chasing the wind. I hated everything I had worked for on earth. I'll have to leave all of it to someone who lives after me. And who knows whether the person will be wise or foolish? Either way, he or she will take over everything on earth I've worked so hard for. That doesn't have any meaning either. So I began to lose hope because of all of my hard work on this earth. A person might use wisdom, knowledge and skill to do his or her work. But then that person has to leave everything owned to someone who hasn't worked for it. That doesn't have any meaning either. In fact, it isn't fair. What do people get for all this hard work on earth? What do they get for all of their worries? As long as they live, the work they do is nothing but pain and sorrow. Even at night, some of them can't sleep. That doesn't have any meaning.

A person can't do anything better than eat and drink and being satisfied with their work. I have finally realised that those things also come from the God. Without His help, who can eat or find pleasure? God gives wisdom, knowledge and happiness to the person who pleases Him. But to a sinner He gives the task of gathering and storing up wealth. Then the sinner must hand it over to the one who pleases God. That doesn't have any meaning either. It's like chasing the wind.
(Ecclesiastes 2:17-26)

Conclusion

Now all has been heard; *here is the conclusion of the matter: Fear God and keep his commandments, for this is the whole duty of human beings on earth. For God will bring every deed into judgment, including every secret thing, whether it is good or evil.* (Ecclesiastes 12:13-14)

TIPS

1. Money and possessions are useful when on earth but all of them are left behind, when one moves on to eternity so don't acquire wealth at the expense of your soul and spirit.
2. Animosity shown to gain positions in life are not necessary remember, that position will not be yours forever.
3. Anything that exult itself higher than the knowledge of God becomes a sin. Wisdom is to assist you to find your way to eternity not to point you to the opposite direction.

The Bible explains that in the spiritual realm, {not visible to the physical eyes} there is God, The Creator and also Satan. Human beings on earth either consciously or subconsciously, report to one or the other.

God made human beings in *His* image to have fellowship and communion with Him. The nature of mankind therefore, is to have fellowship with "A Supreme Being". As such if a person, out of her own free will decides not to relate to God, consciously or unconsciously, that person has given free access to Satan in her life. One thing you have to know is that Satan, just like a thief does not need your permission to (enter) fellowship and communion with your human spirit. In the spiritual realm there are only two main "Beings" God "the Creator" and Satan "the deceiver".

The most miserable place to be, is not fully participating in the evil pleasures of this world, nor accepting God's way of living which leads to spending eternity with Him. Many are those who want to be neutral but the word of God makes it clear that, in eternity, there are, no places for the lukewarm. The following passage clearly points out the dangers of standing as a neutral person in the spiritual realm.

"To the angel of the church in Laodicea write: These are the words of the Amen, the faithful and true witness, the ruler of God's creation. I know your deeds, that you are neither cold nor hot. I wish you were either one or the other. I am about to spit you out of my mouth, because you are lukewarm". *[Revelations 3:14-16]*

The reason why it is so dangerous to be a neutral person in the spiritual realm is that, it makes you vulnerable to every wind of doctrine. This is why in this day and age there are so many different kinds of religion. The Word of God gives a caution in the following passage.

"Until we all reach unity in the faith and in the knowledge of the Son of God and become mature, attaining to the whole measure of the fullness of Christ. Then we will no longer be infants, tossed back and forth by the waves, and blown here and there by every wind of teaching and by the cunning and craftiness of men in their deceitful scheming. Instead, speaking

the truth in love, we will in all things grow up into him who is the Head, that is, Christ". [Ephesians 4:13-15]

Another danger for being a neutral person in the spiritual realm is that you might not be able to discern the actual spirit, behind "spiritual gifts". It is not every spiritual healing and prophecy, which is from God and to be able to have discernment you need Christ. The Word of God gives a warning of allowing ourselves to be used by other spirits in the following passage.

"Many will say to Me [Jesus] on that day, [day of judgement] Lord, Lord, have we not prophesied in Your name and driven out demons in Your name and done many mighty works in Your name? And then I will say to them openly, I never knew you; depart from Me, you who act wickedly by disregarding My commands".
[Matthew 7:22-23]

The Bible helps us to understand, it is not possible to *serve two masters*. [Matthew 6:24]

The forbidden fruit, narrated in the book of Genesis [Genesis3: 1-7], in other words, was the commandment of God on how the woman had to live her life. Eve, being the first woman ever to have lived on earth, was ignorant of the issues pertaining to righteous living and being, which God had intended for mankind.

In a nutshell, God, by *His* infinite wisdom, put all the "Do not" in a fruit and commanded the woman not to eat, or even touch, it. He knew that in succumbing to personal gratification and material wealth, *His* innocent children would be corrupted.

The passage tells us that, as soon as they [Adam and Eve] had finished eating the forbidden fruit, disobeying God's command, their eyes were opened. They became aware of the reality of issues pertaining to living a successful life.

The fate of mankind was changed on that day. Human beings, who were created to have constant fellowship with God, began hiding because of disobedience.

This forbidden fruit can be likened to the Ten Commandments, given to Moses for the Israelites, (and many generations to come) as described in the book of Exodus.

The commandments, just like the instructions given to Adam and Eve in the Garden of Eden, contain the things they should refrain from in order to have a successful life here on earth. Yet a great number of us remain in "disobedient" and hidden from God.

For example let us analyse the 7th commandment [Exodus 20:14] that says, "You shall not commit adultery". Adultery is simply sleeping [having sex] with a man or woman that is not your husband or wife. Most women or men, who disobey this commandment out of their own will are choosing to obey Satan and have fellowship with *him* instead of God. Adultery or fornication, (from the outside)—just like the forbidden fruit—looks "pleasant and good to eat" from the sinner's point of view, but let us look closely at the damage it can cause.

The woman who commits adultery, is not only disobeying God's command, but she is doing harm to her own self and missing out on a fulfilling life, planned for her by her Creator.

Being a follower of Christ or obeying the Commandments of God does not automatically guarantee that life on earth will be glorious, but the spiritual destruction that awaits the woman who commits adultery is devastating, compared with the sacrifice, made in being obedient to God's word.

The teachings of Jesus helps us to understand that, whatever we do out of faith and love, we will surely receive our reward if we are able to endure to the end.

The Beatitudes

Blessed are the poor in spirit, for theirs is the kingdom of heaven.
Blessed are those who mourn, for they will be comforted.
Blessed are the meek, for they will inherit the earth.
Blessed are those who hunger and thirst for righteousness, for they will be filled.
Blessed are the merciful, for they will be shown mercy.
Blessed are the pure in heart, for they will see God.
Blessed are the peacemakers, for they will be called sons of God.
Blessed are those who are persecuted because of righteousness, for theirs is the kingdom of heaven.

Blessed are you when people insult you, persecute you and falsely say all kinds of evil against you because of God. Rejoice and be glad, because great is your reward in heaven, for in the same way they persecuted the prophets who were before you. [Matthew 5: 3-12]

The wages of sin, which is awaiting the woman who sin or commits adultery, can be classified into two main categories, namely, the immediate and the after effects, of sin.

IMMIDIATE EFFECTS OF SIN

Time management for this type of woman is always a problem. Precious time, that could have been utilised to achieve a career, knowledge or something beneficial for future use, is invariably wasted on a relationship, which in most cases ends up in disgrace.

For this woman, managing her finances is also, in most cases a problem because she always wants, to be seen to be dressed in the latest fashion. Sometimes, to keep up with the cost of this lifestyle, not only does she sleep around with other men but also, steals and commits all kinds of immoralities to fund her lifestyle.

Wasting of God—given gifts and talents for this woman is inevitable because she has neither the time nor patience to discover who she really is and the role she is meant to play in her home, her community and in this world.

The woman described above, has a problem bringing her children up properly. The time she should spend encouraging her children, training and praying for them so they don't miss God's plan for their lives, is wasted as she is absent, seeking personal, empty and often fleeting pleasures.

To this type of woman, gambling with her home and her life is a daily event. The day she is caught, the things done in secret will be made known to many. This, in most cases will cost her marriage and bring disgrace to her home.

AFTER EFFECTS OF SIN

Sleeping with a man, outside your own marriage, causes spiritual bond known as soul—tie (a feeling of intimacy which is false).

These ties or feelings for other men, beside your husband, needs to be stopped, or broken in effect through "fasting"(or abstinence), prayer and counselling if the nightmare – and guilt which will ultimately follow is to be avoided. If you are not fulfilled through the relationship with your husband alone, you stand to loose him.

An unwanted pregnancy is also a common result of committing adultery. Unwanted (but innocent) children are aborted everyday due to this immoral act.

Some women, following abortion become infertile as an unfortunate side—effect of the operation. This can bring misery and heartache to a marriage where children are subsequently wanted.

Epidemics of sexually transmitted diseases are also something to worry about.

A study of just one African country shows that, every day, around 1500 people are newly infected with HIV. It is believed that one quarter of the population in that country are already HIV- positive and there is no sign that the rate of infection is slowing down.

A woman who commits adultery causes more damage to herself than she can ever imagine. This immoral practice causes emotional damage, not only to her, but also to the man involved – not mentioning their respective families. The Bible explains this as follows:

Self-destruction

"For the prostitute reduces you to a loaf of bread, and the adulteress preys upon your very life. Can a man scoop fire into his lap without his clothes being burned? Can a man walk on hot coals without his feet being scorched? So is he who sleeps with another man's wife; no one who touches her will go unpunished. Men do not despise a thief if he steals to satisfy his hunger when he is starving. Yet if he is caught, he must pay sevenfold, though it costs him all the wealth of his house. But a man who commits adultery lacks judgment; whoever does so destroys himself". [Proverbs 6:26-32]

To help clarify the plan of Salvation for you and your household, God sent his only begotten Son, our Lord and Saviour to give us power through the Holy Spirit and take us through the master plan.

The forbidden fruit, or the commandment of God, is what Satan presented to Jesus just before his ministry on earth. Unlike the woman in Genesis (Eve) Jesus passed the test giving hope to women of this generation. The passage below, from the gospel of Matthew, explains it as follows:

"As soon as Jesus was baptised, He came out of the water. Then heaven opened to him, and He saw the Spirit of God coming down like a dove alighting on Him. Then a voice said from heaven. "This is my own dear Son, with whom I am well pleased"

Then the Spirit led Jesus to be tempted by the devil.

Then the devil came to him and said, "If you are God's Son, order these stones to turn into bread"

But Jesus answered "Human Beings cannot live on bread alone but need every word that God speaks."

Then the devil took Jesus to Jerusalem, the Holy City, set Him on the highest point of the Temple, and said to Him, "If you are God's Son, throw yourself down, for the scripture says; God will give orders to His angels about you; they will hold you up in their hands, so that not even your feet will be hurt on the stones"

Jesus answered, " But the scripture also says do not put The Lord your God to the test" Then the devil took Jesus to a very high mountain and showed Him all the kingdoms of the world in all their greatness. "All this I will give you, if you kneel down and worship me"

Then Jesus answered, "Go away Satan! The scripture says, worship the Lord your God and serve only Him". Then the devil left Jesus and the angels came and helped Him". [Mathew 3 and 4]

After the baptism of Jesus, the Spirit of God, which came down on *Him*, gave Him power to resist Satan and his cunning ideas. In a similar way, as soon as a person prays the sinner's prayer and accepts Jesus, the Spirit of God [Holy Spirit], empowers that person to resist Satan. Though deliverance from Satan is instantaneous, the battle to keep *him* away is fought daily, through reading the word of God and prayers.

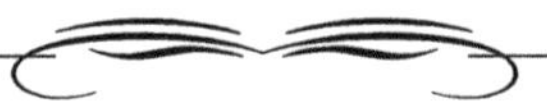

Chapter Nine

SATANS PLAN
KNOWLEDGE
HUMILITY
SALVATION
FAITH
BOLDNESS
THINGS TO REMEMBER

SATANS PLAN

Satan came to steal, to kill and to destroy, and he knows that once the virtuous woman is captured, the whole family can easily be destroyed. This technique is exactly what he used at the beginning of creation to destroy the first family {Adam and Eve}. But, to women of this generation, the revelation received from God for you is that; "*You cannot continuously listen to the dictates and lies of Satan if you want a better lifestyle for you and your household*". God is also saying; "*You cannot solve all the problems in your home, in your community, or in this world, but walk with me and I will give you the power to play your part, for with me all things are possible*".

Ever since the spiritual fall of human beings in the garden, of Eden the woman has always passed the full blame to Satan. "*The Lord God ask the woman, "Why did you do this?" She replied, "The snake tricked me into eating it*". (Genesis 3:13)

But God is saying to the virtuous woman of this generation, "*Before you can fully possess your land, before you can fully take what belongs to you in Christ Jesus, the woman has to stop complaining for a moment about Satan and his cunning ideas, her husband, her children and look at herself*".

God is saying, "*Your responsibility is not to change anyone, but to love and pray for people*". Remember, God has given each individual free will to choose life or death. You can influence a child's mind, but once that child reaches adulthood you can only advise, encourage and pray for them to make the right choices in life.

You should not waste your energy trying to change your husband or your grown—up children because God has not given you that "power" and you will only end up being frustrated.

Understanding of this simple rule will help you to live in harmony with even the most difficult person on earth. Prayer and love are the only keys that will unlock the door to happiness in your homes, communities and churches.

The word of God says, "*Do not judge others, so that God will not judge you, for God will judge you the same way as you judge others, and he will apply to you the same rule you apply to others. Why then do you look at the speck in your sister's [brother's] eyes, and pay no attention to the log in your own eye? You hypocrite! First take the log out of your own eye, and then you will be able to see clearly to take the speck out of your sister's [brother's] eye". [Matthew 7:1-5]*

Virtuous woman, it has been established that Satan is cunning and he is even in the game of working through your loved ones to get to you, but what God is saying is that; "*If you are not careful, you will be caught up in the trap of shifting blame and pointing the accusing finger at others, rather than accepting responsibility for your own shortcomings.*

The Bible has helped us to understand that "*For all have sinned and become short of the glory of God [Romans 3:23]. "If we confess our sins, he is faithful and just and will forgive us our sins and purify us from all unrighteousness [1John1: 9].*

Virtuous woman, before you can partake of the grace God has made available to you and your family through His Son Jesus Christ, there are five fundamental things, you should observe in your everyday life.

KNOWLEDGE

For the Word of God says, "My *people perish for lack of knowledge*" *[Hosea 4:6]*

Knowledge, as some people say, is power. If a child sees a flickering flame, she may be attracted to it, even though she doesn't understand the risk she faces of burning herself. If the same child grows up and understands the uses of, as well as dangers that fire present, she will not deliberately touch it with her bare hands. The reason being, she is now aware of the consequences that will be the result of such actions.

The facts that you do not have a personal relationship with Jesus and you do not understand the reason for your being alive, at this time will neither save you, nor prevent you from being accountable for your actions, at the end of your time on earth.

Therefore, to obtain mercy to know who you are in Christ and to find out why you have been created, building up your knowledge of God and *His* Son should be a priority. The scripture says, "*Stupid people have no respect for wisdom and refuse to learn*".

As a woman of wisdom and understanding, your priority in life should be to know the word of God, so that you can fight the enemy—and win.

For the 21st century woman, acquiring knowledge should not be a problem at all. There are so many different versions of the Bible currently in print. There are also many good books (and tapes) on sale which accurately interpret the word of God. Lastly, as a child of God you have The Teacher (The Holy Spirit) who dwells within you to explain and teach you all things in the Bible. All you need to do is make the time for studies.

HUMILITY

The Word of God says, "*The fear of God is the beginning of all wisdom*"*[Psalm 111:10]*

The knowledge of God will bring you to a place of repentance. It will help you to understand that "*...all have* *sinned and become short of the glory of God*" [Romans 3:23]. From the moment you are born, even though it seems impossible that you could have committed a sin, the Bible says; "...*you are a sinner*". Humility will give you the grace to accept that human beings, by nature are sinful. This sinful nature can be grouped into two main categories; conscious and unconscious sin.

Unconscious sins are those inherited from your parents and forefathers. This sinful nature was passed on to you through no fault of your own but by the grace of God; provision has also been made to wipe it away. All you need to do for your part is to humble yourself before God and receive *His* pardon.

Conscious sins are those committed deliberately through stubbornness but ignorance of the extent of the consequences. A sinful act set in motion, if not broken by the power of God, will complete the full circle. A teenage girl, for example, might be ignorant of the full implications of fornication. This sinful act, if not checked, can lead to unwanted pregnancies or even abortion. The unnecessary destruction of a viable foetus, which would otherwise have developed into a happy productive member of society were it not for that initial sinful act.

Stupidity, as the word of God tells us; "... *is like a loud, ignorant, shameless woman. She sits in the highest part of the town, and calls out to people passing by, who are minding their own business: "Come in, ignorant people!" To the foolish she says, "Stolen water is sweeter". "Stolen bread tastes better." Her victims do not know that people die when they go to her house, that those who have already entered are now deep in the world of the dead. [Proverbs 9:13-18]*

Knowing the word of God will give you the grace to be humble and to flee from conscious sins.

As a virtuous woman, your humility is not only towards God, but also to those, in authority over you; your husband—who is the spiritual leader in your home, manager at work, and your elders in church.

The Bible says, "*In the same way younger people must submit to your elders*".

[1 Peter 5:6] "*And all of you must put on the apron of humility, to serve one another, for the scripture says, God resists the proud, but shows mercy to the humble". Humble yourself, under God Almighty's hand, so that He will lift you up in His own good time.*

SALVATION

Having humility will allow you to kneel in prayer with no thought of shame or embarrassment, to repent and receive grace to obtain salvation, which is a free gift from God.

Salvation is a free gift, but one has to renounce evil and accept Jesus Christ as The Lord and Master of one's life. This is done simply, by confessing with your mouth to God, that you have sinned. Asking Him to forgive you and cleanse you of your sins. Salvation can also be achieved by asking for the assistance of the Holy Spirit in order to live a life of victory.

After the initial confession of your sins and acceptance of Christ as your personal saviour, salvation is also a daily walk with God until the end of your days. The Bible says; "*Walk your own salvation with fear and trembling*", [*Philippians 2:12*] and this means, getting to know God and spending time in prayer in order to fulfil your God -given vision, should be a daily exercise.

Salvation, (as I look at it) is like a gift box that is handed to each and every human being at the 'new birth', {after confessing your sins and accepting Christ into your heart). In this parcel are all the things the person needs to complete his or her journey, e.g. – wisdom, strength, faith, compassion, the plan and purposes of that individual's life, 24 hour help line to communicate with God, and having the Holy Spirit to assist in everything.

This means that Salvation, is personal and as such, no one can obtain it for you, even if they try. The only way to obtain salvation is by accepting Jesus Christ as your personal saviour. The Bible clearly says, "*unless a person is born again*"{saved} *he or she cannot enter the kingdom of God*", [*John 3:3*]. It is therefore a passport, the right to become a citizen of heaven (God's kingdom).

FAITH

The Bible defines faith as follows:—*Now faith is being sure of what we hope for and certain of what we do not see. This is what the ancients were commended for. By faith we understand that the universe was formed at God's command, so that what is seen was not made out of what was visible. And without faith it is impossible to please God, because anyone who comes to him must believe that he exists and that he rewards those who earnestly seek him. [Hebrews 11:1-3 & 6]*

The grace to receive the promises of God is through faith. After Adam and Eve sinned against God in the beginning, God prepared another package for the woman and her family. The only way to obtain all these promises is by having Faith in God.

Provision to supply your needs, has been made available in the package of Salvation but virtuous woman, God is saying; "*To obtain it, there is something you have to do in return and that is to have faith in Him*".

At the beginning, when the devil appeared to Eve at the Garden of Eden, in the form of a serpent, Eve listened to him because she didn't fully exercise her confidence in God. To have faith in somebody is to trust and believe fully in, that person. For example, the reason why you get up every morning and go to work is that you believe and trust your employer to pay you at the end of the week or month your salary. With this trust, belief and expectation, rain or shine you are always on time to perform your duties.

The reason why you eat the meal placed before you, without asking questions, at a restaurant is that you trust the chef and the waiters. You trust them simply because it is a restaurant and the food looks palatable. You completely trust strangers, with your life to satisfy your needs, simply because of outward appearances; that can be deceptive.

Virtuous woman, the word of God from the above passage states that; "*...faith is being sure of what we hope for* (*in* God) *and certain of what we do not see*" (His promises). This means—We have to believe in His word the same way we trust and believe in people. According to the Bible, Spiritual thing, are as real as things we see in the physical.

If Eve had fully trusted God, she wouldn't have listened to the lies the enemy presented. Remember, the enemy is always there to suggest another plan, but it is entirely your choice, to listen to God; by reading His word or by listening to the dictates of your mind and the voices of darkness.

BOLDNESS

Having faith in God will give you the boldness needed to fulfil your God given destiny. If you fully believe and trust that God rewards those who diligently seek *Him*, you will not allow anything to stand in your way.

The grace to be bold is available, but you have to allow your human spirit to grow, by reading God's word and having a personal relationship with *Him* through prayer. When your human spirit is convinced of your Creator, nothing in the physical world can convince you otherwise. Boldness to put into practice what you read from the word of God is acquired not in a day; But by continuously, exercising your faith in God. "Practice" as some people say, "makes perfect" and just like in the physical, spiritual things are also learned in stages. You need to read or listen to the word of God and to believe in what you have learned before you can practice it.

For example, learning how to walk happens in stages; first the baby has to sit, crawl then stand before she can walk. Spiritual matters are learned in the same manner; a baby in Christ, after being "born again" or delivered from the kingdom of darkness into the Spirit of Truth, will first have to learn the word of God, then speak the word of God, before she can boldly exercise her faith in the ways of God.

Why is it so important for the virtuous woman to sort herself out first and get it right with God? The answer is, "Virtuous woman, God has an assignment for you to finish."

THINGS TO REMEMBER

- The woman has to decide whether she wants to take the wide road [which leads to destruction] or the narrow road, which leads to life eternal.

- God has a plan for mankind but so does the devil.

- The forbidden fruit, when eaten, has both immediate and after effects on the woman

- Knowledge of God and humility will bring repentance, which will lead to Salvation – Gods free gift to mankind.

- Faith and boldness will enable you to fulfil the plan God has for your life.

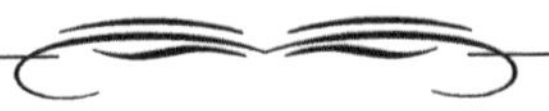

Chapter Ten

THE DIVORCE RATE
TIME FOR EVERYTHING
GOD'S CASES AGAINST MANKIND
NOAH'S GENERATION
MOSES'S GENERATION
ABRAHAM PLEADING WITH GOD
GOD'S JUDGEMENT
THINGS TO DO

The role of a man in any family is important, but we should not underestimate the role of a woman nor the diverse talents given to her by The Creator Himself. The woman, who has the ability to carry her unborn child for nine months, has also been given many hidden characteristics, which enables her to successfully endure, protect and care for her home. Satan is aware of this fact, once he is able to get through to the woman, the whole family can easily be captured and destroyed. The word of God says; " *Homes are made by the woman*". *[Proverbs 31:19]*

Virtuous woman, remember you have been created to constantly find solutions to problems, and not to add to them. You have been made in such a way that with the help of the Holy Spirit, you can survive in difficult circumstances. You have been given the power to travail through prayer until you find a way to change whatever difficult situation you find yourself in for the better. Remember, a loser is a person who quits, you are meant to work out solutions that will take you through the darkness of problems until you come out successfully into the light. You are a valuable asset to your home, community, church and to this world, so be courageous and keep your cool, for the Lord your God is with you. Virtuous woman don't be discouraged by your setbacks. Satan knows your value and that is why he wants you. Once you fall into his claws he will devour you and your household in no time.

The woman should understand that God Himself has ordained the hatred between Satan and her. The war between the two of you is a survival of the fittest.

Virtuous woman is either you put him [the devil] in his rightful place [by feeding on the word of God so that your human spirit can withstand his cunning ideas.] or he will destroys you, and the people around you.

Hatred between the Woman and Satan

God declaring war between Satan and the woman when He said: -

"I'm declaring war between you and the Woman, between your offspring and hers. Her offspring will crush your head, and you'll bite her offspring's heel."
[Genesis 3:15]

Once Satan 'bites the heel' of a person, whether in the physical or in the spiritual realm that person becomes disorientated and death is inevitable if help does not arrive soon.

God, Who declared war between the devil and the woman, has also made provision, through the Holy Spirit, for the woman to always prevail, whenever there is confrontation. What the woman has to do is, accept this truth and have faith in the word of God.

Satan, who was once close to God, was thrown to earth from heaven, due to pride. Satan, who had wanted to be equal to God, fell short of the mark, and ever since then, has been trying all avenues to even it out with God, without success.

Satan's underlined agenda is not only destroying mankind but to fight his enemy [God] with every weapon he has including you and your household.

Human beings are his targets and he still deceives people, to be proud and to think of themselves, (their own knowledge) more highly than the knowledge of God. The Bible clearly says; "*God opposes the proud but gives grace to the humble.*"*[James 4:6]*

This means, anyone who rejects His word [Jesus] is teaming up with Satan.

Satan knows that God loved mankind, so much so that *He* even sent *His* only begotten Son, to die at the Calvary cross, for their salvation. He knows the pain he causes God, anytime he is able to capture a woman or members of her household, and this is why the battle has intensified.

Ever since the lie was told in the garden of Eden, God, by *His* infinite wisdom, has been trying from generation to generation to give back to the human race The Original Plan, (which is having victory over Satan on earth, achieving the purpose for your life and spending eternity with Him). But it seems the virtuous woman has still not fully come to terms with her role. Believe it or not, God is counting on you to stop the enemy and to put an end to *his* cunning ways.

Sometimes, due to frustration, confusion or discouragement, it is either the woman finds herself, listening to the lies being presented once more by the enemy, or she retreats back and does nothing. What she forgets sometimes, is that the thoughts God has about her, her family and mankind, are not evil but they are good thoughts, willing them to spend eternity with Him. The plan, and purpose, God has for each family is so perfect that it is impossible to succeed without *His* help. Remember, a successful life without God does not exist in eternity.

The Almighty God is saying; "Virtuous woman arise and shine for it is not yet over."

The Glory of Zion

"*Arise, shine, for your light has come, and the glory of the LORD rises upon you. See, darkness covers the earth and thick darkness is over the peoples, but the LORD rises upon you and his glory appears over you. Nations will come to your light, and kings to the brightness of your dawn. Lift up your eyes and look about you: All assemble and come to you; your sons come from afar, and your daughters are carried on the arm. Then you will look and be radiant, your heart will throb and swell with joy; the wealth on the seas will be brought to you, to you the riches of the nations will come. Herds of camels will cover your land, young camels of Midian and Ephah. And all from Sheba will come, bearing gold and incense and proclaiming the praise of the Lord. All Kedar's flocks will be gathered to you, the rams of Nebaioth will serve you; they will be accepted as offerings on my altar, and I will adorn my glorious temple. [Isaiah 60:1-8]*

This age is very evil but with the help of the virtuous woman God will once again reveal the Master Plan in every family in every city in the whole world and gather the nations together to Himself.

THE DIVORCE RATE

According to the national statistics in one country, based on 2002 data, the divorce rate is over 40%. In some societies, over 55% of children are recorded to be living with single parents.

Another report shows the percentage of married adults has decreased to 62% from 72% between 1970 and 1990 and that 50% of first marriages are likely to end in divorce.

In the Western world, studies show that unwed mothers, bringing up children on their own, have replaced the traditional two parent family. It is also stated that children of divorced parents suffer problems throughout life, often doing worse at school than the offspring of married couples, and in most cases seeking love and attention in the wrong places, leading to more divorces or anti—social problems in adulthood.

If we are concerned about teenage pregnancies, illegitimacy, run-away dads and children in poverty, then we can no longer ignore the common denominator behind these problems and that is what God, by *His* infinite wisdom wants the virtuous woman to understand and share with others.

The above statistics are not intended to discourage the virtuous woman, rather they are meant to encourage her to find out the real reasons why single—motherhood, marital infidelity, alternative lifestyles and sexual promiscuity are on the increase in our society and to start praying for God to intervene.

Nor should the facts and figures discourage the virtuous woman, who is bringing up her children alone, they should strengthen her and provide a tool with which to fight the enemy: for the word of God "says", "My *people perish for lack of knowledge*".

My people are destroyed from lack of knowledge. Because you have rejected knowledge, I also reject you as my priests; because you have ignored the law of your God, I also will ignore your children. [Hosea 4:6]

God wants the woman to take her place in destiny and to intercede for her children, her home, community and for the whole world, until she sees a change. The word of God says, "Prayers of the righteous avail much".

Therefore confess your sins to each other and pray for each other so that you may be healed. The prayer of a righteous man or woman is powerful and effective. Elijah was a human being, just like us. He prayed earnestly that it would not rain, and it did not rain on the land for three and a half years. Again he prayed, and the heavens gave rain, and the earth produced its crops. [James 5:16-18]

Her prayer for her children should be: -

"I am a child of God.
I am the righteousness of God in Christ Jesus
No weapon formed against my children and my children's children shall ever prosper.
Any evil or negative words spoken over my children I destroy in the name of Jesus.
I plead the Blood of Jesus over my children (Satan is afraid of the name and the blood of Jesus).
I prophesy, on each of my children—They shall walk in the plan and purposes of God for their lives and fulfil their God given destinies.
Thank you God, for answering my prayers", *Amen.*

The virtuous woman needs to be wise, to arrest the demonic powers set in motion against her household and to break the cycle, the enemy has set for her children in the name of Jesus.

For the Bible tells us; "*We are not fighting against human beings but against the wicked spiritual forces in the heavenly world, the rulers and authorities and cosmic powers of this dark age." [Ephesians 6:12]*

This age is what is described as the "dark age", according to the word of God, the virtuous woman has to rise up and assist spiritually in the overall plan God has for mankind.

Virtuous woman, the word of God for you is to fasten your seat-belt and stand your ground because the age in which you live is evil and the enemy has, never since the creation of this world, been so serious to destroy your seed and your home.

Time for everything

God is saying:—

"Everything that happens in this world happens at the time I choose sets the time for birth and the time for death, the time for planting and the time for harvesting the time for killing and the time for healing,

the time for tearing down and the time for building. I sets the time for sorrow and the time for joy, the time for mourning and the time for dancing, the time for making love and the time not to make love,

the time for kissing and the time for not kissing. I sets the time for finding and the time for losing, the time for saving and the time for throwing away, the time for tearing and the time for mending,

the time for silence and the time to talk. I sets the time for love and the time for hate, the time for war and the time for peace". [Ecclesiastes 3:1-8]

Virtuous woman, this is your time to battle through intercession, for your children, your family, your city and your nation, because the age in which you live is very evil.

The enemy is trying to capture as many families as possible to destroy. Virtuous woman, the revelation I have for you is that, run with the vision, God is giving you, for this is a new day and God is about to do a new thing. The enemy has deceived so many people but God is saying with your help, your obedience and your commitment, I will revoke the curse.

Virtuous woman God is saying, "Come and let us reason together." God wants to state His case first and all

He wants you to do, is to listen carefully and see if there is any truth in it: -

God's, cases against mankind

"Heaven and earth, you're the jury. Listen to God's case: I had children and raised them well, and they turned on me.

The ox knows who's boss, the mule knows the hand that feeds him,

But not Israel [My people] My *people don't know up from down. Shame! Misguided God—dropouts, staggering under their guilt—baggage, Gang of miscreants, band of vandals* My *people have walked out on me, their* God, *turned their backs on* The Holy *one of Israel, walked off and never looked back. Why bother even trying to do anything with you when you just keep to your bull-headed ways?*

You keep beating your heads against brick walls.

Everything within you protests against you. From the bottom of your feet to the top of your head, nothing's working right. Wounds and bruises and running sores-untended, unwashed, un-bandaged.

Your country is laid waste, your cities burned down. Outsiders destroy your land, while you watch, reduced to rubble by barbarians.

Daughter Zion is deserted-like a tumbledown shack on a dead-end street, Like a tarpaulin shanty on the wrong side of the tracks, like a sinking ship, abandoned by the rats. If God hadn't left us a few survivors, we'd be as desolate as Sodom, doomed just like Gomorrah." [Isaiah 1:2-9]

God is saying: "*You are one of the few survivors to stop your homes, your communities as well as the whole world from destruction just like Sodom and Gomorrah so what are you going to do about it*"?

Now your question might be "what shows that the age we live in is evil?"

For this generation, God is saying;-

"*My anger is revealed from heaven against all the sin and evil of the people whose evil ways prevent the truth from being known. I will punish them because what can be known about Me, is plain to them. For I Myself, made it plain. Ever since I created the world, Mine invisible qualities, both My eternal powers and My divine nature, have been clearly seen; they are perceived in the things I have made.*

So these people have no excuse at all. They know God but they do not give Him the honour that belongs to Him, nor do they thank Him; instead their thoughts have become completely nonsense and their empty minds are filled with darkness, they say they are wise but they are fools; instead of worshipping immortal God, they worship images made to look like mortal human beings or birds or animals or reptiles.

And so I have given those people over to do the filthy shameful things their hearts desire, and they do shameful things with each other. They exchange the truth about Me for a lie; they worship and serve what I have created instead of The Creator himself; who is to be praised forever! Amen".

Because they do this, God says, "I have given them over to shameful passion. Even the women pervert the natural use of their sex by unnatural acts. In the same way the men have given up natural sexual relationships with women and burn with passion for each other. Men do shameful things with each other and as a result they bring upon themselves the punishment they deserve for their wrongdoing.

Because these people refuse to keep in mind the true knowledge about Me, I have given them over to corrupted minds, so that they do the things that they should not do. They are filled with all kinds of wickedness, evil, greed, and vice; they are full of jealousy, murder, fighting, deceit, and malice. They gossip and speak evil of one another; they are hateful to God, and insolent. Proud and boastful; they think of more ways to do evil; they disobey their parents; they have no conscience; they do not keep their promises, and show no pity for others. They know that God's law says that people who live in this way deserve death. Yet, not only do they continue to do these very things, but also they even approve of others who do it. [Romans 1:18 – 32]

Virtuous woman, God is saying "If you still don't agree that there is something wrong and that this age is evil, then stop being passive, take the time to look around you. God is saying, "*Now what do you see?*" The following cases will help to support my opinion.

Case 1
People have refused
to acknowledge God as the Creator.

These days, in most schools, it is a taboo for children to say the Lord's Prayer, in case they offend somebody who is not a Christian. Christianity, which is meant to be a personal relationship with God {your Creator}, has been given a label, another name known as "religion". And in the name of religion, so many innocent lives have been ruined.

People don't even take the time to explain to their children who made the sun to rule by day and the moon to take over by night. As if they don't even have the time to explain, that the heaven above and the earth below was the handy-work of a Supreme Being.

People have got a scientific way of explaining almost everything that God has made.

Scientist have formulated a theory which explains evolution, they can provide data which goes as far back as the creation of this world to back up their myth which explains that man comes from ape. Unfortunately, if one asks where father and mother ape originated from—that they do not have a tangible answer.

God is saying that people of this age believe in anything, they believe in man—made theories and in everything He [God] has created, but when it come to *Him*—The Creator himself—that is when the problem starts.

Case 2
People do not have any regard for the word of God.

These days, as if to insult The *Creator*, human beings will pair up with anyone rather than follow the order, which the Creator intended for mankind.
[Genesis 3:22-25].

The word of God says:—"*Furthermore, since they did not think it worthwhile to retain the knowledge of God, He gave them over to a depraved mind, to do what ought not to be done*. [*Romans1: 18*]. The fact that you have decided to live your own lifestyle does not mean you will not be accountable for your actions, at the end of your days.

There are so many sexual transmitted diseases around but to some it is all very normal, "part of life", as some would say.

All sorts of crimes are on the increase yet some people, spend their whole lives inventing "evil" such as drugs which makes people "high", boost their self image, and leads them to commit crimes (such as rape, stealing or murder).

Prisons are full of people who believe strongly in the lifestyle, which put them there in the first place. The love of their 'sinful' lifestyle is so strong that even after their release and so called rehabilitation, they often return to the same routine.

Case 3
Children lack knowledge of the word of God

Children in today' s society often lack respect for authority figures, parents, teachers, police, never mind God, who is not visible. Some of them threaten, abuse, and even kill their parents and teachers. They start drinking, taking drugs and indulging in different forms of crime before they can even tie their shoelaces and woe betide anyone who wants to challenge their way of reasoning!

The word of God says; "*train a child the way they should go*" and "*they shall not depart from it when they grow up*" [*Proverbs 22:6*].

The madness in some of them can trigger in a day – and that means somebody seen to be normal one day is capable the next day of picking up a gun and killing people with no regard for human life. Some of them grow up to be adults before society realises what monsters they have helped to create.

Case 4
We live in self—centred and materialistic world

Truly the Bible say; "*The love of money is the root of all evil*". What won't people of this age do for money? The age in which we live is so self—centred, and so materialistic, that people will use others as ladders to climb up the social ladder, without giving their feelings a second thought. Some people simply, do not have any regard for other human beings. It is all about "survival of the fittest", and the attitude of, "I am more important than you ". These attitudes, of self-centredness and hatred for others are in our homes, our work places, in the society and spread throughout the world.

Case 5
We are losing our spiritual, moral, and cultural values

These days, most of the films that are produced, books that are published, and songs that are written, have lost their spiritual and moral value. The wisdom to understand nature, in the Word (Bible) to be passed on from generation to generation, is also losing its value. It has been replaced by the advertisement of the "evil" from which people should turn away. This generation is falling, deeper and deeper, into a bottomless pit.

Virtuous woman these are some of the few cases I believe God, has against this generation and *His* question is; "*Are you going to stop being passive and do your bit to solve these problems or not*"

The question, I am sure you want to ask next is "*Why are evil, and the lies, more attractive to this generation*"?, than the truth and knowledge of God.

To find out why evil and lies are more attractive to this generation, that God and truth, we must first look at the economic and political set up in our societies and in our nations. In order to survive in any society, or in any nation, one has to abide by the rules and regulations laid down by the governors of that land.

To understand this point correctly we need to go deeper than the physical and identify the powers, which influence those placed in authority, to make rules in our nations.

Virtuous woman, God, wants me to inform you that, " *Be aware of the powers that are ruling this world*". The Bible has made us aware that Satan was once very close with God Almighty, but he was proud and couldn't accept that he was less than God. Because of his pride, he was cast down, from heaven to earth.

"The king of Babylonia, bright morning star, you have fallen from heaven! In the past you conquered nations, but now you have been thrown to the ground. You were determined to climb up to the heaven and place your throne above the highest stars. You thought you would sit like a king on the mountain in the north where the gods assemble. You said you would climb to the tops of the clouds and be like the 'Almighty', but instead, you have been brought down to the deepest part of the world of the dead.

The dead will stare and gape at you. They will ask, is this the man who shook the earth and made kingdoms tremble? Is this the man who destroyed cities and turned the world into a desert? Is this the man who never feeds his prisoners or let them go home?" *[*Isaiah 14:12-17*]*

God really wants you to understand this revelation:— The first part of this prophecy, was fulfilled before the creation of this world. Satan, because of pride and wanting to compete with God, was cast of heaven to dwell below on earth for a season. When he came down he brought a great deal of baggage; – pride, disrespect for The

Creator, wanting to get followers to prove his importance, criticising and testing God, to discredit Him.

Unlike Eve in the Garden of Eden, the woman of this generation has help available. The Lord Jesus Christ has already defeated the devil, your duty, is simply accept this fact and hold on to this revelation – for this is the only passport you need, to declare to the enemy that you are not part of his kingdom.

Virtuous woman your next question might be "Why is this generation worse, or different, than past generations"?

God wants you to understand *His* nature and the way in which *He* has dealt with unrepentant generations since the beginning of time. Take a look at the following two major incidents in the Bible and the curses that were imposed on them as a result.

'NOAH'S GENERATION'

This is the story of Noah; he had three sons, Shem, Ham, and Japheth.
He lived in fellowship with God, but everyone else was evil in the sight of God and violence had spread everywhere. God looked at the world and saw that it was evil, for the people were all living evil lives.
God said to Noah, "I have decided to put an end to the whole human race, I will destroy them completely because the world is full of their evil deeds."[Genesis 6:9-13]

Virtuous woman, because Noah heard *His* voice he spared him and his household and gave them back the original plan of life including all the animals, which were created in the beginning, to start again.

God then promised that "Never again will all *living* things be destroyed by flood, never again will flood destroy the earth."

God wants you to understand that when a generation is out of control through evil judgement and destruction is inevitable, but never again is *He* going to use the same method twice.

'MOSES'S GENERATION'

To make it easier, for mankind to follow *His* Master Plan, *He* handed Moses the Ten Commandments on Mount Sinai.

And guess what, while Moses was receiving the necessary instructions, to carry out his duty to lead that generation back to God, the devil showed up once again—with the duplicate plan.

When the people saw that Moses had not come down from the mountain but was staying there a long time, they gathered round Aaron and said to him "We do not know what has happened to this man Moses, who led us out of Egypt; so make us a god to lead us
The Lord said to Moses, "Go back down at once, because your people whom you led out of Egypt, have sinned and rejected me. They have already left the way that I commanded them to follow; I know how stubborn these

people are. Now don't stop me. I am angry with them and I am going to destroy them. And I will make you and your descendants into a great nation
Moses saw that Aaron had let the people out of control to make fools of themselves in front of their enemies. So he stood at the gate of the camp and shouted.
"Everyone who is on the Lord's side come over here!" So all the Levites gathered round him and he said to them, "The Lord God of Israel commands everyone of you, to put on his sword and go through the camp from this gate to the other and kill his brothers, his friends and his neighbours". The Levites obeyed and killed about three thousand men that day" [Exodus32: 1-28]

Virtuous woman, God wants you to understand his nature. When a generation becomes evil or out of control, he pronounces judgement but does not use the same method twice. For this reason, if you see brothers killing themselves or neighbours killing each other in the name of religion, God wants you to be aware that, it is not *His* fault because, since the beginning of time He promised not to use the same method twice to destroy people for their evil doing.

Virtuous woman, what God means is, *He* is about to do something new, *He* is about to come down *Himself*, to see if this evil on earth is true, and bring judgement but just like Abraham, you can choose whether to be part of it [an intercessor pleading for mankind] or to opt out of the whole process. I believe for this generation, God is saying:—"*I know how stubborn these people are. Now don't stop me. I am angry with them and I am going to destroy them".*

Abraham pleading with God

"When the men got up to leave, they looked down toward Sodom, and Abraham walked along with them to see them on their way. Then the Lord said, "Shall I hide from Abraham what I am about to do? Abraham will surely become a great and powerful nation, and all nations on earth will be blessed through him. For I have chosen him, so that he will direct his children and his household after him to keep the way of the Lord by doing what is right and just, so that the Lord will bring about for Abraham what he has promised him."

Then the Lord said, "The outcry against Sodom and Gomorrah is so great and their sin so grievous that I will go down and see if what they have done is as bad as the outcry that has reached me. If not, I will know.

The men turned away and went toward Sodom, but Abraham remained standing before the Lord. Then Abraham approached him and said: "Will you sweep away the righteous with the wicked? What if there are fifty righteous people in the city? Will you really sweep it away and not spare the place for the sake of the fifty righteous people in it? Far be it from you to do such a thing to kill the righteous with the wicked, treating the righteous and the wicked alike. Far be it from you! Will not the Judge of all the earth do right?"

The Lord said, "If I find fifty righteous people in the city of Sodom, I will spare the whole place for their sake."

Then Abraham spoke up again: "Now that I have been so bold as to speak to the Lord, though I am nothing but dust and ashes, what if the number of the righteous is five less than

fifty? Will you destroy the whole city because of five people?"
"If I find forty-five there," he said, "I will not destroy it."
Once again he spoke to him, "What if only forty are found there?"
He said, "For the sake of forty, I will not do it."
Then he said, "May the Lord not be angry, but let me speak. What if only thirty can be found there?"
He answered, "I will not do it if I find thirty there."
Abraham said, "Now that I have been so bold as to speak to the Lord, what if only twenty can be found there?"
He said, "For the sake of twenty, I will not destroy it."
Then he said, "May the Lord not be angry, but let me speak just once more. What if only ten can be found there?"
He answered, "For the sake of ten, I will not destroy it."
When the Lord had finished speaking with Abraham, he left, and Abraham returned home".[Genesis 18:16-33]

God is saying, "*I* have promised since Noah's days, that *I* am not going to use the same method twice to punish people for the evil they do. I am not going to command brothers who are for me, to kill their brothers who have turned against me, nor am *I* going to ask neighbours who are for me, to kill other neighbours who are doing evil. God is saying, *As a matter of fact I don't want you to even pass judgement on your brothers, husbands or neighbours, because I also have something against you, you who are called my children, who are meant to be my friends*".

God's Judgement.

You, therefore, have no excuse, you who pass judgment on someone else, for at whatever point, you judge the other, you are condemning yourself, because you who pass judgment do the same things. Now we know that God's judgment against those who do such things is based on truth. So when you, a mere man, pass judgment on them and yet do the same things, do you think you will escape God's judgment? Or do you show contempt for the riches of His kindness, tolerance and patience, not realizing that God's kindness leads you toward repentance?

But because of your stubbornness and your unrepentant heart, you are storing up wrath against yourself for the day of God's wrath, when his righteous judgment will be revealed. God will give to each person according to what he has done. To those who by persistence in doing good seek glory, honour and immortality, he will give eternal life. But for those who are self-seeking and who reject the truth and follow evil, there will be wrath and anger. There will be trouble and distress for every human being who does evil: first for the Jew, then for the Gentile; but glory, honour and peace for everyone who does well, first for the Jew, then for the Gentile. For God does not show favouritism.

All who sin apart from the law will also perish apart from the law, and all who sin under the law, will be judged by the law. For it is not those who hear the law who are righteous in God's sight, but it is those who obey the law who will be declared righteous. (Indeed, when Gentiles, who do not have the law, do by nature things required by the law, they are a law for themselves, even though they do not have the law, since they show that the requirements of the law are written on their hearts, their consciences also bearing witness, and their thoughts now accusing, now even defending them.) This will take place on the day when God will judge men's secrets through Jesus Christ, as my gospel declares.

[Romans 2:1- 16]

Virtuous woman, the part you have to play is not too demanding, thanks to our Lord and Saviour, Jesus Christ. All you have to do is find out what part you need to play in the great plan of Salvation and play it well.

For in every evil generation, God always looks for one righteous person with whom to make a covenant. He then reveals *His* Master Plan for creation and asks this righteous **person to share** the plan with those willing to listen, who will be willing and obedient to carry out the specific instructions given, so that they can survive the destruction and pass on the plan of life to the next generation.

THINGS TO REMEMBER

Virtuous woman, God wants you to understand that whilst the preparation for saving the righteous is going on, all those who do not change their ways and partake of the instructions given by God for survival, will have no choice but to perish for their sins. But the question here is, "How many people are you prepared to intercede for, to help find their way?"

Secondly, "Have you taken the time to discover why you are here at this present time? Have you discovered your use in God's big plan for salvation?" It could be that you have not discovered the valuable talent, which God has given you and, as such, you think of yourself as useless. Virtuous woman, it's never too late, get on your knees and talk to your Creator until *He* provides the instructions for your life. God has a plan and a purpose for every individual on earth.

Thirdly, remember, Jesus Christ came down to earth to show you how to make it through the journey of life.

With Him you cannot fail. In the kingdom of God there is no failure, you might not be on top of the "social ladder" in your society but you might be what all creation is waiting for to get mankind on the right path.

Virtuous woman, look for women who are carrying the same vision to see a change. Meet on regular basis and intercede for the problem and challenges you are being faced with. Remember, any obstacle you come across in life is a stepping-stone for you to progress. God is counting on you to get the work done and you cannot afford to let Him down. Remember, power to work out solutions to problems has been given to the woman and this is achieved through the Holy Spirit.

Whatever you need on this journey of life remember, God knew about it before you were even formed in your mother's womb, but the only way to get answers manifested in the physical realm is to get into *His* word and find out what you have to do to invoke that blessing to 'fall 'on you.

Finally, remember that whatever you do has to be backed-up with your faith. The word of God says, "*Without faith, it's impossible to please God*" [*Hebrews 11:6*], so surround yourself with inspiring teachings of God and listen to good Christian music that will build your faith up daily. The Bible says, "*Faith comes by hearing the word of God*"[*Romans 10:17*]

Feed on the word, for you know not when the enemy will come knocking on your door. "Even Jesus Christ, had to use the word to dismiss Satan".

Then Jesus answered, "*Go away Satan! The scripture says, worship the Lord your God and serve only Him*".

Then the devil left Jesus and the angels came and helped Him [Matthew 4:10].

In all you do remember, it's not by might, nor by power, but it's only by The Spirit of The Living God and with God all things are possible!

God is looking for yielding vessels [women] to pour Himself into, to accomplish end time prophecies!

THINGS TO DO

- If you don't know how to use something, you will treat it with levity. Find out why you have been created and what part you have to play in God's plan.
- Find out what irritates you most in life because it's a sign you can do something about it.
- The age we live in is folding—up so this is the time the woman has to spread the message and intercedes for her home, community, and the world as a whole.
- The enemy is very angry, roaring like a hungry lion, to devour the woman and her seed, so rise up and put up a fight to stop him.
- You cannot solve all of the world's problems as well as your own but you can be part of the solution.
- God is depending on you to count for eternity so arise and shine.

  Be on guard, stand true to the truth you believe in, be strong and courageous and let love be your primary focus in everything you do.
- Virtuous woman take your place in destiny.

Lucy is a woman of destiny and I know she was brought into my life by divine arrangement.
She is a woman who, through life's challenges, has been prepared to make an impact on her generation.
Indeed this book has done that and it will impact and push women into their destinies at a time like this, when women are called and destined to be a solution to today's problems facing society especially the family.

Deaconess Jessie Sampar

Lucy takes pleasure in bringing out the best in people, especially women. She has written this book, packed with revelations from deep spiritual truths to enrich and encourage women from all walks of life who wish to discover the virtue in them.
God comforts us in all our troubles so that we can comfort others who in turn are troubled themselves.
Lucy is ministering through her life experiences and I pray God will bring healing and deliverance to anyone who takes the time to read this message.

PRAYER PARTNERS
(Modupeh, Miriam, Eunice and Camilla)

Mum won't allow the blanket of everyday life to shield and prevent her from finding the real truth and "meaning of life". Whereas others prefer to remain in their 'comfort zones' and not strive to attain answers to questions such as, "Why am I here?" "What is life about?" believing, there are no set answers; Mum is one of the few people who will put themselves 'out there' in order to find the truth, even though it's the more difficult path to follow.

Jeff

If you enjoyed reading this book, please look forward to another road map to Destiny.

That he might present the bride to himself a glorious church, not having spots, or wrinkles, or any such thing; but that it should be holy and without blemish.

- As Christ loved the church
- Sanctification
- Spots and Wrinkles
- Blemish
- The Glorious Bride

www.ingramcontent.com/pod-product-compliance
Ingram Content Group UK Ltd.
Pitfield, Milton Keynes, MK11 3LW, UK
UKHW040015200726
13854UKWH00001B/209

9 781412 026321